A HANDBOOK OF JAZZ

a handbook of JAZZ

by Barry Ulanov

THE VIKING PRESS   NEW YORK   1960

FOR ANNE

contents

contents

preface

A whole new generation has grown up in jazz since I last wrote a book about this subject, less than a half-dozen years ago. Generations grow up quickly in jazz, whether of musicians or of fanciers of the music. The newest of the jazz generations has much to learn about this art, about its past performers and the places in which they played and the people who came to hear them play. The older ones have much to learn about the newest, too, about its personalities and predilections and those who are pleased by both the men and their tastes. One of the basic purposes of this book is to perform the necessary introductions, to bring the generations together in jazz. It is important, I think, to suggest to those who find their pleasure in the music of New Orleans or Chicago in the opening decades of this century, or of Kansas

City and New York in the thirties and forties, how much is to be found in the jazz of the boppers and the cool generation and the neo-classicists. It is equally vital to acquaint the followers of Charlie Parker and Lennie Tristano, of Jimmy Giuffre and the Modern Jazz Quartet and all the others of like modernity, with some of the facts of jazz life to go with their fancies.

History, then, plays a central role in this book. But the lines of historical development provide only one set of references in jazz. There are all sorts of cross-references in this music: the schools to which the various musicians belong, the instruments they play, the language they speak, the records they have made, the way they look at their own performances and the way others—professional critics or amateur—do. As many as possible of these points of reference have been brought together in this compendium to form what might almost be called a geometer's-eye view of jazz. Finally, that this view might have still further depth, the reader is offered a comparative chronology with which to compare the key events in jazz and allied arts in the twentieth century. It is instructive to see just how closely related is the development of these other arts to jazz. Yes, one must at least make the effort to see jazz in depth, for depth, at this point, jazz surely has.

BARRY ULANOV

A HANDBOOK OF JAZZ

1 jazz then and now: a capsule history

The jazz world is a small world; it would be dishonest to call it anything more. But to all those who love it and work in it, it is, of the many small worlds of the universe of the arts, the most prepossessing, the most complete, the most—well, that is exactly what a jazz musician would call it—"the most!"— and let it go at that.

It has always been thus in jazz. From the very beginning —whenever that may have been, and wherever—jazz has commanded of its performers an extraordinarily single-minded loyalty and dedication. To understand jazz one must understand this. To this devotion, this concentration of everything upon what must seem to many merely another music— and not so fine a music at that—to this, only the zeal of a fanatic can be compared.

Jazzmen are zealots, they are fanatics; but their fanaticism has about it a grace that softens their wild enthusiasm, even at times tames it, and their zeal does know some bounds—the bounds of art. Jazz musicians have always worked hard to learn their instruments, to get to know them better and better; they have in fact made them their familiars. But for once familiarity has bred respect—a respect for horns and the notes one blows upon them, for the discipline and control of the art of music, of which jazz is today so vital a part.

The precise time and place of the beginnings of jazz are not known, nor will the most tireless efforts by researchers uncover this sort of information with any exactness. All that we know of the origins of jazz is a general culture pattern; all that we really have is a sense of background, a series of directions into the past. The pattern is clear enough: it is crazy-quilt, marvelously disorganized in the American fashion, with a sense of order to be found only through a squinting of the eyes or a view from a great distance. Seen in long perspective, the parts make sense. There are church music, music of the fields and the work camps, the marches to and from the burial grounds, music out of the hills, and before that music from England and Scotland and Ireland and France and Germany; and over it all a beat, a driving beat, that may or may not have been brought over in the slave ships from West Africa.

It is clear that all this music went into the patterns of culture in the Southern states. It would be wrong to omit the work songs, for example—the rhythmic accompaniments of field workers, and of workers who laid down the railroad lines, those who were called "gandy dancers." Church music in the South, the development out of well-known denominations and of many that are obscure, of a hymn with a beat, of the spiritual, something very close to the blues—that is a fascinating part of the story. And finally, as one turns to the plantations and the big-city slums, moves through church choirs and chain gangs, looks at every sort of dance and listens to the Voodoo rites, one must account for the African origins, no matter how remote, of the musicians who first played jazz.

The harder one listens to jazz, the more one hears European rather than African influences—the folk songs of England, Scotland, and Ireland, of France and Germany and even the Balkans, rather than the music of the jungle and the coast settlements from which the slave ships came. Theoretically the connection with Africa is attractive, romantic, not altogether unpersuasive; to the ear it is only the most dubious of ancestries. The characteristic rhythmic complexity of African music has never been approached by jazz. Only in very recent years has anything like it been attempted by jazzmen, and then by musicians who have had no remote connection with Africa and whose music has almost nothing in common with the multiple and quite unmeasurable beats of a corps of African drummers.

What matters, it seems to me, is not what parts came together to make up the jazz pattern, or where or when it happened, but that they did in fact come together, that they make sense together, and that as early as we have any record on paper or in phonograph-record grooves, this music has an identifiable manner, and something of the matter, which today we associate with jazz. And this, after all, we do know with certainty: that in the 1880s in and around New Orleans, and in other parts of the South, they were beginning to play the music we call jazz; that for all its resemblances—and they were many—to the several different kinds of music from which jazz sprang, this music was beginning to take on the characteristics of a homogeneous art form.

Jazz arose from its surroundings, then, as any primitive art does—spontaneously—with little or no awareness on any-body's part that something new was being born. The early musicians of jazz were obviously quite content to employ the instruments and the tone system of conventional Western music. To their borrowings, however, they added much: a simple piety all their own, a certain amount of protest, an occasional poignancy, a characteristic irreverence, an anti-sentimentality, that pervade all the first jazz of any import-ance. The dreariest, most pompous or pretentious jazz per-formance has a flippant turn of phrase here, a frivolous counter-statement there, little patches and snatches of irony that give any music that is worthy of the name of jazz a robust if not a ribald flavor.

The first performers in jazz are figures more of legend than of life: the singers and instrumentalists who reached back to the twelve-bar form of the folk tune, to its simple chord structure and typical melodic line, combined these with the texture of the Negro spiritual and other elements less easy to identify, and evolved that most durable and most thoroughly adaptable of jazz forms, the blues. There is little question, in my mind at least, that long before the famous early names of jazz—before Buddy Bolden and Freddie Keppard and Papa Laine, before Ma Rainey and Bessie Smith, before the Original Dixieland Jass Band and the New Orleans Rhythm Kings, before King Oliver and Louis Arm-strong—there were men and women in the backwoods and the front parlors making the delicate little changes, insisting upon the famous "blue notes" (flatting the third and seventh notes of the scale) without shifting key. These were, I think, the fascinating folk of early jazz, those who imposed order upon it, who set perhaps for all time the infinitely flexible form, the three-phrase (A-A'-B) form, of the blues, susceptible of endless lyric and melodic variations. These were the amateur musicians who gave to jazz that first essential emphasis on improvisation. Among these early experimenters, too, there must have been the first who expressed discontent with the polite sounds normally made on the brass horn, the cornet, the wind bass, the trombone, on the honky-tonk piano and even on the drums. For from among these anonymous amateurs came the impetus to develop little bands for Storyville (the red-light district of New Orleans) and for all the other across-the-tracks quarters in Southern and Southwestern towns where they were beginning to play jazz in the late years of the nineteenth century.

The small bands developed alongside ragtime, and were much influenced by but not necessarily evolved from the same sources as the piano rags. Ultimately, the two kinds of music came together; by the end of the First World War everybody who played ragtime in America also played jazz, and vice versa. But earlier, in the late years of the nineteenth century and the first of the twentieth, ragtime was a more disciplined music than jazz, for all its resemblance to the louder, less controlled music that was being played down the street. The first ragtimers of quality, such as Scott Joplin and Tom Turpin and Louis Chauvin, were capable of an elegance, an organization of melodic resources and harmonic textures which their jazz counterparts could not conceivably match. What ragtime contributed to jazz in its brisk forays up and down the piano keyboard, in its nervous little four-bar breaks and sometimes dignified sixteen-bar choruses, was a respect for a complete command of instrumental technique and an understanding of the place a composer could have in a music which was largely improvised. These valuable contributions and a repertory of rags that could sustain almost any kind of improvisational mayhem give ragtime an important place in the early history of jazz.

Jazz did not reach records until the Original Dixieland Jass Band recorded for Victor in February 1917, and therefore the most durable documents of this music are comparatively recent. There are other documents, however: the various guides to the houses in the Storyville district, which provided not only an unofficial directory of the *"dames de joie,"* but also some of the first mentions of the names of the jazz musicians who played in the bordellos; newspapers contemporary with the first jazz bands in New Orleans; reminiscences of the early jazz musicians published over the years in the jazz magazines; the loving research of jazz historians and the not-quite-so-affectionate chronicles of writers about the not-so-old South who could not help giving jazz a chin up or a kick down. From these sources and others we know now that King Oliver and Sidney Bechet, Emanuel Perez and Oscar Celestin, Alphonse Picou and Jelly Roll Morton, were all Storyville performers in the years just before the district was shut up by the Secretary of the Navy in 1917 in order to free servicemen of its pernicious influence. We know about Buddy Bolden's band with its cornet lead, clarinet and trombone following after, and bass, guitar, and drums keeping the rhythm going, which about 1900 became the fixed pattern for jazz-band performers. We know about the marching bands, the St. Joseph brass band, the Excelsior, the Eagle, and the Olympia; through all of them styles and stylists filtered, giving shape and form to that music which just after World War I we associate properly enough with two large figures, the trumpeters Joseph King Oliver and Louis Armstrong.

They played much of this music on the river boats, men like Louis, and Pops Foster the bass player, Baby Dodds the drummer, Picou the clarinetist, and the pianist Fate Marable. But what made jazz permanent was the arrival in Chicago of King Oliver and all the bands that derived from his, and the success, first in Chicago and then in New York, of the white jazz bands, Tom Brown's Dixieland Jass Band and the Original Dixielanders.

The Brown boys were actually Papa Laine's musicians, graduates of his Reliance Band and others which that brilliantly successful contractor of music for New Orleans had led or organized. Tom Brown and his musicians played at the Lambs Café in Chicago to increasing crowds. So did the Original Dixieland Jass Band when it moved from the Casino Gardens in Chicago to New York, first to Bustanoby's and then to Reisenweber's. How many of these musicians, or of those who made up the New Orleans Rhythm Kings in Chicago in 1920, are of enduring importance in jazz? Not many, but the playing procedure they helped to institute in jazz is enormously important, for it was immediately imitated all over the United States. Each of these bands, too, always featured a clarinetist of wit or elegance or at least great agility, such as Alcide Nunez, known as "Yellow," or Larry Shields, the best of them, or Leon Rappolo, who might

have been one of the giants of jazz if his mind had not
wandered even more adventurously than his music. The
white Dixielanders had something more than clarinetists—
they had humor; even the most casual listening to the
technically wretched recordings made by the Original Dixielanders and the Rhythm Kings reveals a relentless attack on
sentimental tunes, a fine corny sense of humor, the kind one
associates with the imitation of barnyard noises, and a clown-
ing caterwaul that keeps step as easily as the simple
parade tunes of John Philip Sousa played by a fife-and-drum
corps.

In the decade just after World War I a certain order began
to impose itself upon jazz. The musicians who played the new
music knew one another, listened sympathetically and with
great interest to one another, exchanged advice, and were
conscious, as jazzmen never had been before, that they were
working together to create something of significance, in show
business anyway, something that made reputations, increased
incomes, and brought with it a kind of satisfaction that
transcended financial considerations and fame. Out of King
Oliver's band came Louis Armstrong and the clarinetist
Jimmie Noone, both of whom combined at various times with
Earl Hines, the pianist, to produce the best music to be
heard in Chicago in the early twenties. Louis played for a
while with Fletcher Henderson, the most gifted of the early
arrangers and composers of jazz, who gave the big band some
of the mobility and relaxation of the small, and made it possible for musicians of the caliber of Coleman Hawkins,
Benny Carter, and Louis Armstrong to display their individuality in a setting that enhanced rather than detracted from it.

Henderson also accompanied the great bawling blues singers of his time, Ma Rainey and Bessie Smith and Ida Cox
and many others, giving them a background sumptuous or
simple as the songs required, big band or small, piano and
rhythm together, or piano alone.

The same rewarding collaboration of musicians of quality
is found in the records made by soloists who could from time
to time escape from the frustrations of the so-called "symphonic jazz" associated with Jean Goldkette and Paul Whiteman, into recording studios. There they made free-swinging
catch-as-catch-can jazz blows under Frankie Trumbauer or
Bix Beiderbecke, or with some of those inspired Chicago
youngsters, Frank Teschemacher, Muggsy Spanier, Bud
Freeman, Jimmy McPartland, Dave Tough, Eddie Condon,
Gene Krupa, or Joe Sullivan.

Whether people hated or loved it as the music of "free
love" or as the natural rhythmic inspiration of the new
poetry; whether they fell for the synthetic version that
George Gershwin and Ferde Grofé between them made of
jazz, for the *Rhapsody in Blue,* for Paul Whiteman's 1924
concert at the Aeolian Hall in New York; whether they
agreed with the facile condemnations of jazz as "disgusting,"
"diabolic," "sadistic," or "chaotic" or turned to it with sympathy—whatever the attitude, everyone *did* have an attitude
toward jazz in the 1920s, in the time that will forever be
called in the history of our culture "The Jazz Age." And
with good reason. For the new art of jazz was making its
way into the consciousness of Americans, not only as part
of the poetry of T. S. Eliot, Carl Sandburg, Vachel Lindsay,
E. E. Cummings, not only in such novels as *The Great
Gatsby,* in the music of Stravinsky and Ravel and Bloch,

over the growing radio networks, in night clubs and musical comedies, and on the first sound tracks of the "talking pictures"; it was also beginning to take shape as an independent art form of great eloquence, which permitted the emergence of soloists as different from each other as Louis Armstrong and Bix Beiderbecke, arrangers as thoroughly individual as Fletcher Henderson and Don Redman and Duke Ellington, and singers of such strikingly different styles and backgrounds as Bessie Smith and Mildred Bailey.

There was jazz of quality right across the United States in the twenties. The best of it unquestionably did make its way to records—the settings, for example, that Louis Armstrong's Hot Five and Hot Seven gave him to blow against. Louis and his colleagues quickly put together an imposing repertory of tunes and variations on those tunes, and created a veritable alphabet of phrases and figures, which remained the basic tunes, variations, and catch-phrases of jazz for a quarter of a century or more. Such men as Johnny Dodds on clarinet and Kid Ory on trombone, and later and most important of the group, Earl Hines on piano, turned what started out as a background setting into a mosaic of sparkling solos, which other recording groups could admire but not quite imitate.

There is much of great beauty in Bix Beiderbecke's small-band records, made at almost the very same time as those inspired sessions led by Louis and Earl, but the beauty is almost all in the playing of Bix, in his sweet cornet phrases, his ballads, his ebullient leadership of the New Orleans jazz classics, his unmistakable authority whenever he makes his appearance, never quite matched, not even by the enthusiastic Frankie Trumbauer on the C melody saxophone. There are passages in Goldkette records with Bix, by Joe Venuti on violin and Eddie Lang on guitar, and in various other of Bix's dates with men like Miff Mole on trombone, the Dorsey Brothers, and different members of the Chicago gang, in which some of the pointed precision, mixed with a tenderness that is typical of Bix at his best, is caught and thrown back by an associate or two. For the kind of ensemble Bix should have had, one still turns to some of the swinging sides made in such startling number by Bix's friends and colleagues recording under Red Nichols, the brassman who might be much better known today if it were not for Bix. The cornetist turned trumpeter who organized fine sessions in New York. He brought into the studio such musicians as Jack and Charlie Teagarden, Benny Goodman, Jimmy and Tommy Dorsey, Glenn Miller and Joe Sullivan, and made them all come together in easy harmony, with a marching ensemble that is almost as pleasant to listen to as the solos that emerge from it.

It wasn't only records; it was also ballrooms, in which bands like Fletcher Henderson's in New York and McKinney's Cotton Pickers (under the direction after 1927 of Don Redman) in Detroit and King Oliver's in Chicago turned a tawdry employment into jazz history. And it was night clubs too, especially such New York clubs as the Kentucky and the Plantation in 1926 and the next year the Cotton, where Duke Ellington sat down with the band which to many is still synonymous with jazz. Each of Duke's soloists in the late twenties and all through the thirties and the early forties offers almost the definitive example of what to do with his instrument. Duke's sections—his reeds and his rhythm and his brass—were deployed as no other composer or arranger in jazz had ever organized them, to express the imagination not of one man or six or seven, but of thirteen or sixteen or twenty. This was the final push, the great propulsion of the big bands of jazz, which took the music out of a back-room hum and redeemed what had been to too many just a pleasant background for barroom tinkle and clatter, and made it possible for hundreds of others to make this music their profession and their art.

It was many people, Louis and Bix, the Chicagoans and the New Orleans musicians, Fletcher and the blues singers, Earl Hines and Jimmy Noone, Don Redman—but most of all it was Duke Ellington who set such standards, who gave soloists, collaborators really, such opportunities that now one could talk of values in jazz and not merely of box office. Thus jazz was able to sustain the difficulties of the depression years, to fight off the assaults, intended or not, of a Rudy Vallee or a Guy Lombardo and all their imitators. For from Duke's music came unmistakable echoes of the human personality, evocations of folk sorrowful or jubilant in the growling accents of Tricky Sam Nanton on trombone, and first Bubber Miley and then Cootie Williams on trumpet. From Duke's music came all the astonishing innuendo—astonishing because so inoffensive while it remained insinuating—of Johnny Hodges on alto and Lawrence Brown and Juan Tizol on trombone. From Duke came not just beat, not just color, not just catchy tunes and beautifully polished arrangements, but the freeing hand of the experimental orchestrator. He gave the saxophone section a new depth and breadth in the way he matched alto and baritone saxes; he extended the range of the brass section and made his trumpets and trombones almost into a chamber group within

the larger orchestra; and before he was finished he turned
the double bass free and made it into one of the great solo
voices of jazz.

No other band was as free as Duke's in the late twenties or
the early thirties, or had such a mixture of personalities. But
there was a fetching lilt to such bands as Luis Russell's in
New York, the band that Louis Armstrong used as his background when he came back from several years of enormous
success in Europe in 1935. There was a fine free-swinging
fullness to the band Earl Hines led at the Grand Terrace in
Chicago, as there was to every organization that Earl formed
and led in the thirties and forties. There was a rugged massiveness in the Kansas City music, the music taking shape
under the leadership of Bennie Moten and Andy Kirk, the
music that was later to be associated so indelibly with Count
Basie. And down the road a piece there were the inheritors of
the Whiteman and Goldkette audiences, the bands made up of
musicians who had played with Red Nichols and the Chicagoans or had listened hard to them, the bands led by the
Dorsey brothers and Glen Gray.

The performances of these bands serve to mark the incisive
difference between "white" jazz and its Negro inspiration in
the early thirties. There is much more of quality in the
Dorsey Brothers' recordings than in the Casa Loma band
under Gray; but both outfits suffer seriously from the limitations of that ugly, unwritten, but vigorously enforced social
contract that separated the two races in jazz until the advent of Benny Goodman and swing. Even the best of the
white bands were stiff, unrelaxed; not even the most attentive ministrations of such experienced and roundly talented
musicians as clarinetist Jimmy Dorsey and trombonist

Tommy could bring their orchestras fully alive. Not even the fistful of talent that Ben Pollack held in his drumming-leading hands in the late twenties and early thirties, enough talent later to form two distinguished jazz bands, Benny Goodman's and Bob Crosby's—not even the Teagardens and Jimmy McPartland, Benny Goodman and Glenn Miller and Ray Bauduc could quite bring this music alive. It awaited a change in public mood and private, a new set of arrangers, a new group of front men. Thus the need for, thus the fulfillment, of "swing."

What was responsible for that extraordinary change of mood in the American people that made a whole country so receptive to jazz in 1936? It could have been "The Music Goes Round and Round," as it seemed to so many of us who watched and heard it happen, in that dizzying Christmas season of 1935. It could have been the ecstatic response of audiences at the Palomar Ballroom in Los Angeles to the Benny Goodman band, after it had laid eggs at Billy Rose's Music Hall in New York and at some of its other early appearances. It may have been the hundreds of thousands who had heard Benny Goodman's studio band so many late Saturday nights broadcasting hour-long jazz sets over the NBC network. Or perhaps it was the patrons of the little holes in the wall on Fifty-second Street in New York City, a few leftovers from the speakeasy era and many more youngsters down from the colleges to hear "the real jazz," "the righteous stuff," to see and hear Teddy Wilson and Fats Waller at the piano, Bunny Berigan, Red McKenzie, Wingy Manone, and all the others they had read about or heard on a record or two. To some extent it was all of these things, and an increasing national income as well. But beyond that, and of far greater importance in the history of jazz, it was the joining together of talents of various kinds, white and Negro, some ancient veterans of the early days as old as forty and fifty, and some babies who had not yet reached their majority. It was Fletcher Henderson doing arrangements for Benny Goodman's band at least as good as anything he had ever turned out for himself. It was radio programs wholly dedicated to swing, a term which covered a whole mess of music, some of it more messy than musical, but most of it with the tell-tale beat. It was the collaboration of musicians of all kinds, of all backgrounds, in those thoroughly relaxed and brilliantly varied dates led by Teddy Wilson and Billie Holiday, together and apart, by Lionel Hampton, and by a whole flock of others who did not sustain quality for quite so long or at quite so high a level. It was the fact that jazz was beginning to be written about with much seriousness and even more enthusiasm, that jazz was fit for Carnegie Hall after 1938, when Benny Goodman appeared there, and that fans had begun to take sides in jazz, supporting whole schools or small groups or big bands or single musicians, championing their causes with all the academic equipment, articulateness, and intensity that earlier only baseball had been able to elicit from such large numbers of Americans.

There were deserving causes too. Count Basie's band came to Chicago in 1936 and then to New York, and all by itself, with soloists such as Lester Young, Buck Clayton, Harry Edison, Benny Morton, and Dickie Wells, and with an infectious rhythm section made even more attractive by its leader-pianist's pirouettings in and out of it, established for many the definitive swing sound. It became increasingly clear in the late thirties that Basie's was the high level of this kind of jazz. Other bands, other musicians, could live for a while on the same dizzying plateau on which he and his musicians dwelt, but the atmosphere there was too rarefied for permanent residence, even for such memorable Benny Goodman graduates as Harry James and Gene Krupa and Teddy Wilson. There was a pleasant rough-and-tumble quality to some of Harry's music, and he had a remarkable teen-age tenor saxophonist in Corky Corcoran to feature beside himself, and he and his arrangers and his musicians constructed some thoroughly satisfactory backgrounds to accompany the really quite distinguished singing of Helen Forrest and Dick Haymes, and briefly, earlier, Frank Sinatra; but Harry James' Band was never more than a merely amiable swing organization.

Amiable is the word that best describes the music of Teddy Wilson too, especially after he had had the sense to cut down from the conventional five reed, five brass, four rhythm of a large band to the much more manageable sextet, one of the most facile and flexible sextets in its many years as a fixture, now at Café Society Downtown, now at Café Society Uptown in New York. Gene Krupa's was a powerful personality in front of or behind a band, and with the perhaps even more potent Roy Eldridge and Anita O'Day he made a really distinctive contribution to jazz. Gene went on, with Charlie Ventura and Roy and Anita and thoroughly up-to-date scores, to make a place for his band in the early days of bop, but he, like most of the other Benny Goodman sidemen, never was able to weld his musicians together to achieve the necessary ensemble brightness, the concise attack, the esprit de corps that distinguished Basie's as the best of all the swing bands.

Ensemble spirit as it was never known before, and perhaps never since, was the identifying mark of the Jimmie Lunceford band. Here all that was mechanical in the Glen Gray Casa Loma organization was carried through to something approaching perfection, with the machine oil all but visible. The machine oil? Hours of rehearsal to achieve an impeccable showmanship, both for the eye and the ear. And with the showmanship, there came a remarkable musicianly poise, the result of that heavy, driving two-beat into which such arrangers as Sy Oliver and Eddie Durham had converted Dixieland humors. This wasn't a matter of soloists, though there were some excellent ones such as Joe Thomas on tenor and Willie Smith on alto, but rather of ensemble; it was the mark of Lunceford, it was the mark of dozens of really able swing bands.

Down South, across the Midwest, up and down the West Coast, there were well-rehearsed bands, swinging bands, bands with a good tenorman or trumpeter, a burly trombonist, a brash drummer, or a fleet pianist, any one of whom could at the drop of a downbeat demonstrate incomparable technical skill and incredible rhythmic power. Were their techniques really "incomparable"? Was their rhythmic power really "incredible"? Well, perhaps not individually; perhaps their achievement was not that remarkable, not each man on his own instrument. But en masse, regarded as a unit, no other group in any art in America had ever before established such unmistakable mastery over their instruments, in the normal performance of their regular duties, as did the swing bands.

Up at the Savoy Ballroom in Harlem, for example, there were all those astonishing house bands, regularly responsible, each of them, for the most irregular sort of duty. For six or seven years in the thirties and for almost as many again in the forties, these rambunctious organizations, and others like them, demonstrated that mixture of technical precision and rhythmic power which made the swing era so captivating. From Willie Bryant's band came the natural good humor of its leader. From Teddy Hill's band came soloists like Roy Eldridge and Chu Berry and some of the early formulations of that modern jazz which was to become bebop. From Chick Webb's band came the best beat around, the achievement of the best drummer around, the gallant little leader of the band; and there came from this group too a succession of very able soloists, for Chick, like Fletcher Henderson, was always able to pick them and keep them.

Numerous as the bands of quality were, however, it was not they but the individual musicians that made the swing decade into the classical jazz era, the jazz equivalent of the Elizabethan period in English literature or the seventeenth century in French literature or the nineteenth in Russian. Never before in jazz were so many so good all at once. Never before did so many styles firmly implant themselves in the jazz earth, not even in the days of the founding fathers of jazz. Never before (or since, really) were identities so clearly marked, personalities so pronounced in their effect upon jazz. The list is long, much too long to give in precise detail, but it is important to block out the large figures and fashions that were coming to dominate jazz in the late thirties and early forties, to indicate, instrument for instrument, who meant what in jazz, and to some extent why, in those stirring years.

It was a time of polls, and the polls followed the pattern of the swing band. To begin with, always, it was the reeds. There for many years it was Benny Carter or Johnny Hodges who set solo alto style; and Toots Mondello and Hymie Schertzer who developed that liquid lead alto sound which dominated reed sections right up until yesterday. On tenor, it was a Dixieland sound, an irony, since the pure Dixielander would have no truck with a saxophone, but from Chicago's Bud Freeman and, later, New Orleans' Eddie Miller came a variety of sweet and bubbling tenor lines that hundreds across the United States imitated; and then followed the triumph of the Gargantuan tenor sound of Coleman Hawkins, with its heavy audible breathing, and of the many imitators and disciples, some almost as good as Hawk himself, such as Chu Berry, Ben Webster, and Georgie Auld. All through the swing years and afterward, as a counterpoise to the more flamboyant tenormen, there were the playing and thinking and influence of Lester Young, who undoubtedly owed something to Bud Freeman for his petit-point patterns, and necessarily learned something of how to construct a ballad from Hawkins, but made a tenor style all his own, the most durable of all tenor styles in its cool, compact, close-noted, gently honking perambulations down familiar tunes and chords. Finally in the clarinet section of the band there were Benny Goodman and Artie Shaw, about whose heads and mouthpieces controversy raged for at least half a dozen years. There was controversy about their bands, but Benny's, clearly, was the more important of the two, the incubator of so very much jazz talent. There was controversy about their sounds, Benny's richer and bigger, Artie's perhaps more supple; but it was obvious, too, that Benny's tone and technique and thinking were at once more classical and more generally adaptable to other musicians. There was controversy about the Negro musicians each brought into the white fold, each courageous as men in their position in jazz had never been before, each of excellent taste in the choice of playing associates from uptown or the other side of the city; for Benny it was Teddy Wilson and Lionel Hampton in the early years and Cootie Williams in the later; for Artie Shaw it was Billie Holiday and then Lips Page and Roy Eldridge.

Among the trumpets it was now Benny Goodman's Harry James and Ziggy Elman, now Bob Crosby's Billy Butterfield and Charlie Spivak, now Bunny Berigan, leading his own band or as Tommy Dorsey's brightest star. Able as these men were, however, the great trumpet music in jazz in the swing years was beyond everybody else's Roy Eldridge's, a ripping, tearing jazz, that music played by Little Jazz, who was as endlessly inventive of bright little phrases as Louis Armstrong, but more adaptable to new styles and far more adventurous. Only the brilliant alternation of muted grunts and growls and open-trumpet melodic flights by Cootie Williams could match Roy in intensity and imagination and range.

Among the trombones, for most people, it was Tommy Dorsey, as bandleader, as balladeer, as debonair Dixielander. For many, Jack Jenney or Lawrence Brown performed, in all but the duties of a leader, as well as Tommy; for others, Will Bradley was Tommy's equal in everything. But if one had a taste for a more barrelhouse trombone sound, one preferred Jack Teagarden or J. C. Higginbotham or a little later Bill Harris. And if one's major interest was the resourcefulness of a melodic imagination, then one turned to the considerably less famous but undoubtedly more inspired Dickie Wells of the Basie band in the swing years. For Dickie was the trombone equivalent of Lester Young, wonderfully gifted in constructing lines made up of bouncing notes of brief valuation, of delicate arcs put together very carefully, either a tiny section at a time or in one or two capital sweeps which were the precise match for Lester's protracted honks; it was a matter of musical justice that his elegant little "Dickie's Dream" should have been recorded at the same session by the same small Basie band that performed "Lester Leaps In."

On bass, listeners in the swing years heard men of some real skill but no great imagination, until in 1941 and 1942 Jimmy Blanton remade the instrument, preserving its position as a mainstay of the rhythm section but adding to its stature a full head, a well-filled head, of solo lines. Similarly, the guitar waited for the incisive pluckings of Charlie Christian to turn rhythmic duty into plectral eloquence, to offer guitarists potentialities that were not fully realized until the late forties and early fifties.

Drummers of grace and vigor, steadiness and style—there were plenty of them in the swing years; the drums did not have to wait for the linear manipulations of Max Roach, so much like those of Blanton and Christian, to achieve distinction in jazz. There was Dave Tough, first in outright Dixieland jazz and later in a much more swinging beat, to drive bands and ensembles of all sorts, and to inspire soloists with steadiness and humor, with power and a piquant personality. There was Jo Jones to set up a bright cymbal chatter, if not to maintain quite so much steadiness, with the Basie band and others that borrowed his services. There was the finely mixed assault of the technically solid Buddy Rich, and the authority, the almost aggressive authority, of a large man, Big Sidney Catlett, in some ways the best of all of these drummers.

There was no end to the number of pianists in the swing era, and not just run-of-the-keyboard pianists, but virtuosi and schoolmasters, personalities, stylists. There was the most important of all the founders of schools, Earl Hines; the furious precision of his articulation gave rise to stories of impossible operations on the fingers. "Trumpet-style" piano they called his blasting arpeggios and trigger trills, and his playing did have the vitality of a Roy Eldridge or a young Louis as well as the adventurousness of a young bopper. Out of the groves of ragtime academe and the hustling pedagogy of James P. Johnson came Fats Waller's stride-style piano, the best of all the throwbacks to old New Orleans' playing atmospheres. This style managed charmingly to maintain a beat with the left hand as it alternated single notes and chords, while it permitted every sort of delicate destruction of the sentimental in the trills and tremolos and rippling runs of the right hand. From what Fats took from James P., the rags, the gin mills, and from the capricious Waller imagination, Art Tatum constructed the most significant of swing piano styles. Pianists such as Serge Rachmaninoff and Vladimir Horowitz came to listen and to marvel at Tatum's technique; this was the epitome of elegance at the piano keyboard, in or out of jazz, and those who were the classical opposite numbers of Tatum could recognize, as Art contrived his embellishments with fastidious precision, that this was their kind of mastery. Tatum's ornamental style did more than merely festoon the classics of jazz and salon music; it opened to a new generation of pianists all the challenging possibilities of counter-melody, of counter-statement, of development beyond the restrictions of chorus and chords and convention.

By comparison to Fats and Earl and Art, other pianists were lesser pianists, but a couple of them were of nearly the same importance in the history of jazz. Teddy Wilson, like Tatum, extended considerably the variations upon the well-known playing procedures, in wise and wide left-hand chording, and in lyrical middle-tempo performances of an abiding subtlety of beat and melodic structure. Mary Lou Williams, like Teddy much influenced by Earl Hines, added to incisively articulated keyboard statements the graces of an always active imagination that welcomed anything new in jazz and usually made good use of it.

Singing in jazz in this time went far beyond the bathos of the crooners or the lubricious monotony of the debased blues singers. Mildred Bailey set the standards for band singing, first with Paul Whiteman and then with the orchestra that she and Red Norvo led: she was generously gifted with preciseness of intonation and tenderness of phrase; she could sing with lilt or a larruping good humor, as the song required; she had rhythmic and tonal instincts that could do justice to every one of the able lyrics and better tunes with which a few song writers were providing jazz singers. Ella Fitzgerald, Chick Webb's discovery, showed from a very early age just how well sweetness of sound and of soul could be combined with a natural enthusiasm to make almost any song singable over or under a jazz performance of high— and loud—quality. Finally, in this group of great ladies of jazz, there was Billie Holiday, who scooped pitch, reconstructed cadences, and broke up phrases to make vocal lines of all the enduring beauty of the best instrumental kind.

The male singers, as the polls called them in the swing era (and as a matter of fact still do) were (and still unfortunately are) mostly of the simpering sort. They sang a pathetic repertory of tunes and looked the parts they sang as they draped themselves listlessly round microphones. A few escaped the horrors of the profession and managed at the same time to hold onto their well-filled purses by combining a beat and a virile personality with a respect for all the heavy sighs and staggering gestures of the ballads of unrequited love. Such a singer for a while was Dick Haymes, and such for still longer was Frank Sinatra. Woody Herman turned to a tradition that reached no farther back, really, than Red McKenzie, to compound for himself the most attractive and the most musicianly of these jazz-ballad styles. But for some real indication of what could be done by the male voice in jazz one turned to the high histrionics of Joe Turner or Jimmy Rushing, both masters of the short symmetrical periods of the blues narrative and well stocked, both of them, with a far-reaching repertory. And if one was fortunate enough, one heard from time to time in the realm of scat singing something more than the well-lowered boom of Cab Calloway; one listened, enchanted, to the jabberwocky jive of Leo Watson.

An enormous change was taking place in jazz in the early 1940s, and everybody was aware of it while it was happening. It was being documented, chronicled, noted in detail, almost as fast as the changes of texture, of school, of style, of the whole way of looking at jazz, occurred. Everybody who was attentive to jazz was aware that swing was about at its end, that big bands were almost ready to give way to small, that a new music was ready to take over, and new musicians with it.

Some of the musicians were not that new. Besides the comparatively young Charlie Christian and Jimmy Blanton, both of whom died in 1942 in their middle twenties, there were the veterans Roy Eldridge and Lester Young to set newer and higher solo standards, to lengthen lines, to suggest some of the new conceptions of the new music. And in the big bands of Earl Hines and Billy Eckstine, in which some of the first development of bop as a band music took place, there was a suitable mixture of youngsters and those who had been around in jazz long enough to be called middle-aged, at least in terms of the history of the music and the experience of playing it.

Bop was really a product of Fifty-second Street in New York—the last notable contribution to jazz of The Street—and of Harlem, of Minton's Playhouse in South Harlem, where so many of the ardent young converts to this music were first made. It is unimportant, really, whether bop can be said to have emerged from the small band led by Kenny Clarke at Minton's in 1940 or 1941, or to have been the product of the first sessions in which Dizzy Gillespie participated around New York in the same years, when he was playing with Cab Calloway, or can be tracked back to the playing of Charlie Parker with Jay McShann's booting Kansas City Band at the turn of the decade. The fact is that a new linear conception of jazz was evolving in those first forties; that in melodic lines of a remarkably even scale something of a baroque splendor was attaching itself to the mellifluous alto of Charlie Parker, to the rapid-fire trumpet runs of Dizzy Gillespie, even to bass lines as played by Oscar Pettiford, to some of the tenor playing of Budd Johnson, to many of the melodies invented by the pianist Thelonious Monk, and to the brilliantly accented drumming first of Kenny Clarke and then of Max Roach.

Musicians came from all over to listen and speculate, to disparage or to praise, but never, any of them, to be quite the same afterward. A whole rash of trumpeters, some who had been around for quite a while, some quite new to jazz, turned to the new music, found it very difficult to play with a genuine brassy flavor, and then turned, most of them, to imitating the saxophone lines of Lester Young and Charlie Parker. Among the trumpeters there were some fresh and creative stylists, however. Howard McGhee achieved some very attractive middle-register melodic variations of small compass, of unpretentious charm. Miles Davis, acting and sounding as of he were walking with infinite care over acres of eggshells, played alter ego and alternate solo to some of the best of Charlie Parker's music in the late forties and acted as host and leader for a richly inventive band that featured, among other instruments, tuba, French horn, and baritone saxophone. But the best of all these bop trumpeters was the short-lived Fats Navarro. Gifted with a huge tone and a superb ear, he was as disciplined in his playing habits as he was undisciplined in the rest of his life; the purity of his musical diction is yet to be equaled by any other bopper except Charlie Parker; the precision of his execution was matched only by Clifford Brown, who lost his life in an auto accident just five years after Fats died.

The opposite number of Fats and Cliff on trombone was J. J. Johnson, a sometimes miraculously articulate performer, who restored to the trombone something of the grace it had lost in years of desultory handling by musicians who should have known better or at least could have made an effort to know better. As a result of his playing and that of Bill Harris in a very different groove with the Woody Herman band and of Kai Winding in a similar modern style with the Stan Kenton orchestra, the trombone came alive again in jazz.

All sorts of instruments were given new vitality by the administration of bop lines, by the captivating brilliance of a music that was essentially melodic, far removed really from the chunky rhythms and squared-off harmonies of big-band swing, reaching with an inevitable enchantment to the inner beings of solo-minded jazzmen. A most remarkable renaissance of the guitar, for example, followed upon bop. Banished from rhythm sections by band leaders trying to save money in the difficult musical economy of the war years, the guitar burst forth in new colors as a result of bop, and soloist after soloist demonstrated the freshness of accent the instrument could bring to a small combination. Stan Kenton featured a Brazilian guitarist, Laurindo Almeida, who in a few years turned out to be a perfectly natural complement to the cool formulations of West Coast saxophonists. Later Stan turned to the sweet lines of Sal Salvador for his

guitar solos. Out of the Herman band came the remarkably
steady Billy Bauer, the well-organized Chuck Wayne, the
poetic Jimmy Raney. Two Southerners, Tal Farlow and
Johnny Smith, brought a lovely softness of utterance into
ballad lines. And for sheer incisiveness of guitar sound, there
was—and is—Barney Kessel, much influenced by Charlie
Christian and endlessly devoted to the technical resources
of his instrument.

All across jazz great changes occurred in the years during
and after World War II. The astute leadership of Woody
Herman commanded everybody's attention in jazz from
the mid-forties to the early fifties as he organized and led
band after band of great contagious spirits. The 1944-1946
powerhouse was driven by an impeccable trumpet section
and a rhythm section of high good humor presided over by
Chubby Jackson on bass and first Dave Tough and then Don
Lamond at the drums. The next band, in the late forties,
was an eloquent example of cool jazz, marked by the tenor
sound of Stan Getz and Zoot Sims and the vibe solos
first of Red Norvo and then of Terry Gibbs. Finally, with a
series of changing personnels, there was a band that was
many things in the early fifties, but never less than pro-
vocatively modern in the scores provided by Woody's chief
assistant in his most important years in jazz, Ralph Burns.

Stan Kenton left the impress of his large, lanky, leathery
personality upon jazz in a series of bands that marked perhaps a half-dozen retirements from and re-entries into this
music. A chart of his contributions might very well be a
graph of decibels, of variously noisy and restrained ensemble sounds, the result of variously roaring and relaxed
arrangements. The small philharmonic he organized for his

1950 tour, dedicated to "innovations in modern music," helped, as did so much of Stan's talking and writing and pleading and commissioning and contriving and commanding, to break down opposition to a jazz that knew no limitations of convention and was as adventurous and experimental as its musicians' skills and the record companies' daring would permit.

Another leader who has led his way in and out of bands of distinction is Dizzy Gillespie. Dizzy has clowned a great deal over more than a decade of leading big bands, but he has also often played with a persuasive seriousness, and as his resources have permitted he has gathered around him musicians capable of executing not only his own ideas but those of such imaginative and resourceful arrangers as George Russell and Quincy Jones. It is unfortunate for Dizzy as well as for jazz that he came along at a time when the fixed personnel was no longer easy to establish, to have or to hold.

Perhaps the least self-conscious of all the leaders of important jazz bands has been Count Basie. Suddenly in the mid-fifties, jazz woke up to what this mild-mannered, unassuming man was continuing to do in jazz: like Duke Ellington over so many years, he had proclaimed and was maintaining a standard of performance, of library, of soloists, that made any evening spent with his music at the very least entertaining and at the very best exhilarating, as the band exhibited in set after set its rhythmic vitality in easy-going jazz phrases that burst from time to time into orchestral splendor.

Side by side with the development of bop emerged another music, sometimes closely allied to the jazz of Charlie Parker and Dizzy Gillespie, sometimes at a considerable remove from it. For a while this jazz went by the name of "cool," an adjective well calculated to describe the restraint, the lowering of temperature sometimes almost to the point of frigidity, the change of playing manners and public personality from extravert to introvert. All these elements were germane to any discussion of cool jazz but they did not and they do not adequately define the contribution to jazz of a Lennie Tristano or a Dave Brubeck, a Lee Konitz, John LaPorta, or Gerry Mulligan. Perhaps it is best to say that with musicians such as these, the emphasis in jazz shifted from a reliance upon sheer rhythmic vigor, or overpowering technique, or membership in a going school, to the residual powers that musicians found all at once in their own direct jazz inheritance and in the larger background of classical music to which they now directed their attention. The result was an efflorescence of counterpoint in jazz, of melodic line set against melodic line, all of it put together with a precision and a wit and a wisdom not unrelated to the early rough polyphony of New Orleans but far beyond it in maturity of concept and execution, in freshly meditative musicianship.

Lennie Tristano brought to New York from Chicago in 1946 conservatory training and the personality of a jazz intellectual. Apart from his own pianistic powers, he is a teacher of uncommon magnetism who has been able to summon from the shadows the rich ideas on alto saxophone of Lee Konitz and tenor saxophone of Warne Marsh, among many others. His sometime associate John LaPorta, on alto and clarinet, teaching and composing and arranging, has performed a similiar function with a wide variety of musi-

cians on all instruments. Both Lennie and John have shown
great respect for jazz traditions, but as freeing elements in
their playing and thinking, as springboards for the imagination, rather than as restraining influences.

On the West Coast, schools not unrelated to the Tristano
and LaPorta circles have sprung up in vast number. With
the exception of Dave Brubeck's San Francisco groups, most
of the Coast combinations, fixed or fluctuating, have taken
shape around the formulations of such exiles from the East
as Shorty Rogers and Jimmy Giuffre, Bud Shank and Shelly
Manne, Jack Montrose and Bob Gordon. These musicians,
working in and out of the studios, on records, at sessions of
all sorts, have annoyed many and delighted as many more.
Whatever their limitations, whatever their addictions to this
or that mechanical school of composition, whatever con-
trivances they have seen fit to impose upon their imaginations, they have almost always, with an admirable stead-
fastness of purpose, essayed the experimental, worked hard
and long in the laboratory. And whenever they have failed
at this or that experiment in atonality or counterpoint, in
this or that attempt at new sounds with woodwinds or percussion, they have been able to turn to swinging retorts
that have reminded their listeners once again that this is,
after all, jazz.

It is good to realize, as one looks at jazz in the second
half of the twentieth century, how much experimentation
has come to be taken for granted. There was eager reception,
almost no opposition, on the part of audiences of a dozen
different jazz persuasions, when Gerry Mulligan combined
the most softly inflected of baritone saxes with a trumpet
similarly played (by Chet Baker) and drums and bass,

turning away from the guitar and the piano in the construction of a new jazz chamber music. Nobody thought it particularly strange when Mat Mathews combined the sounds of flute (Herbie Mann) and accordion (Mat) in his quartet. The cello has made its way into jazz in the playing of Oscar Pettiford, in various combinations, and in the work of Fred Katz with the Chico Hamilton Quintet. Jimmy Smith has taken the organ—electronic version—out of the slough of despond (for which read "rhythm and blues"), and has given it thoughtful attention, making it into a jazz voice of unusual depth and brilliance and humor, rarely failing in his solos to take full advantage of manuals and pedals. A similar sort of contrapuntal wit informs the writing and playing of John Lewis on piano and Milt Jackson on vibes in the Modern Jazz Quartet. A far greater reach still is that of the Brothers Sandole, Adolph and Dennis, on manuscript paper and in concert, in impromptu jam and in teaching sessions, with the only limitations those of an innate musicianship, most of it self-tutored, which these two boys from Philadelphia use to punctuate breathtaking little poetic flights across modern jazz.

There are many, many others, who have made modern jazz the enormously stimulating music that it is, not excepting those in Sweden and Germany, France and England, who are very much a part of the jazz of our time. But perhaps the best example of what present-day jazz is all about is to be found in the music of Charlie Mingus, the bass player and composer, arranger, pianist, leader, entrepreneur, and recording director. In all his roles, Charlie is haunted by an image of perfection which he has tried to run to earth—or to recording microphone or nightclub p.a. system, or to manuscript. He is that special mixture of the naïve and the sophisticated which the best jazz musicians have always been. Anti-sentimental and carefully guarded most of the time in the defense or development of an idea in music, no matter how little tried or understood, he will give all of himself to a jazz performance and take as much as he can get of somebody else. With every sort of technical skill on the bass, he has gone on from where Blanton left off, making his most brief appearance in a band performance a provocative commentary on the music at hand. Alternately eloquent and tongue-tied with words, Mingus (as he is best known to friend and foe alike) has the conviction that some day he can make his ideas perfectly clear on his own instrument or somebody else's. He knows, no matter how wispy these ideas may appear to him or to others, that some day it will be possible to give them musical definition—and in jazz. For he has lived, in two decades in the business and art of music, to see all sorts of ideas achieve expression in jazz. He, like so many others, has been a participant in and witness of the development of an art form out of the very simple materials of a form of popular entertainment. He has seen and heard what was once a music of two- and four-bar phrases grow large enough to express something of the full dimensions of the human personality.

2 the instruments of jazz

No jazz musician would accept the following definition made by the English physicist Alexander Wood in his book on *The Physics of Music:* "Musical sounds are those which are smooth, regular, pleasant, and of definite pitch. Unmusical sounds are rough, irregular, unpleasant, and of no definite pitch." All jazz musicians would agree with Wood that "the classification is only approximate at the best." As a matter of fact, the word "approximate" would not be strong enough for a jazz musician. For in jazz, while pitch is respected, every sort of approach to it and away from it has been taken by instrumentalists and singers; and roughness and irregularity and what is normally called unpleasant often have positive values in this music.

None of this is to say that jazz musicians do not understand

and respect their instruments, but quite the contrary. Because they know the potentialities and negotiable values of their horns, brass or silver or gold; because they recognize what can be done beyond the routine employment of the guitar plectrum; because they have seen and heard and used so much of the large resources of keyboard instruments, they refuse to yield to fixed definitions of normal playing procedure and strict limitations of the range and color of their instruments. They are not foolish enough to believe their instruments are without limitations, but like runners resolutely attacking the time it takes to negotiate a mile, half-mile, or lesser distances, they are determined that for a long while to come the limits will be those of lung or lip or finger rather than of valve or mouthpiece, of string or pick or stick.

It is actually because of the willingness of the first jazz musicians to experiment with the richness and color of their instruments that from its very early days this music has taken on textures quite unlike any other. A characteristic quality of jazz is the kind of growl and grunt of which the trumpet and trombone are capable. The fullness of the upper register on the brass instruments as played by jazzmen, the sinuousness of the saxophone in jazz, and the remarkable range of tones to which even an instrument so precisely limited as the piano may attain when played by an adventurous jazzman—these are the definitive sounds of jazz.

TRUMPET

In the beginning jazz was played on the instruments, chiefly, of the brass band: cornet, clarinet, trombone, wind bass or tuba, and drums. Other additions in those early days were the banjo (or occasionally the guitar) and the piano, the participation of which was necessarily excluded from most parades or trips around a Southern city on the bouncing back of an advertising wagon. From fairly early days on, the trumpet alternated in use with the cornet, until, at least during the swing era, it looked as if the cornet were being banished from jazz altogether. There are still some musicians, however, who recognize the sweet tones of which the cornet is capable and prefer it, as a result, to the more searing, more brilliant trumpet. With either instrument the comfortable range is from E or F below middle C on the piano to the C two octaves higher, with something close to an additional octave variously available to those remarkable trumpeters who can pierce the sound barrier.

TROMBONE

The trombone in jazz, as in any other kind of music, offers its performer the challenge of manufacturing his own pitch, even as any string instrument which has to be tuned before (and often during) a performance. When played in tune it extends an octave below the trumpet to F and goes to the G above middle C. Like the trumpet's, the range of the trombone has been extended considerably in the hands of dexterous performers whose lung power and precision of lip match their deftness in fingering the positions of the slide.

TUBA

The tuba really designates, in the music of our time, a family of instruments rather than any one single horn—all those wonderfully scrambled examples of the boilermaker's art that go by such names as the Euphonium, the Sousaphone, the wind bass, or that most imaginatively designed of all tubing assemblies, the horn properly called the tuba. For all practical purposes the range of these instruments in jazz has been accepted as that of the string bass, that largest of the instruments of the violin family, which in its great gruff tones sounds an octave lower than the notes written for it and, tuned in fourths, begins its mellifluous ascent from the E scored two octaves and a sixth below middle C.

CLARINET

First of the several reeds to make their way into jazz was the B-flat clarinet, which ranges from D below middle C to the C two octaves above it. Ironically enough, now that the rational, evenly spaced Boehm fingering system has almost entirely replaced the awkward old Albert system, the clarinet has almost passed out of jazz. Nonetheless, though chiefly performed by virtuosi associated with the swing epoch (Benny Goodman, Artie Shaw, Buddy De Franco) and such amiable Albertians of New Orleans origin as Barney Bigard and Edmond Hall, it still intrigues a few redoubtable moderns, musicians like Tony Scott and John LaPorta.

GUITAR

To complete the instrumentation of the first jazz bands, mention should be made of the four-string banjo (G-D-A-E), a well-plucked and strummed rhythm instrument which sounded an unmistakable four-four beat. Alternating for a while with the banjo, especially as a solo instrument, was the guitar, which replaced its round cousin in the rhythm sections of the swing bands and still retains an important solo role in jazz, although it is not found so often in rhythm sections any more. The guitar as used in jazz is a six-string instrument (E-A-D-G-B-E) which starts an octave higher than the bass and reaches to the E just above middle C.

SAXOPHONES

The great change effected in jazz instrumentation after the dispersal from New Orleans was the addition of the saxophones, one by one. These instruments, created by a Belgian, Adolphe Saxe, have been with us since the middle 1840s and have been enormously successful in this century as a result of their employment in jazz and in all Western music of a popular nature since the end of World War I. In jazz, the major saxophones are the alto (in E-flat) and the tenor (in B-flat); the first ranges from D-flat below middle C to F an octave and a fourth above middle C, the second from A-flat an octave and a third below middle C to E-flat an octave and a third above middle C. The B-flat soprano saxophone reaches an octave above the tenor; the B-flat bass an octave below. The E-flat baritone extends an octave lower than the alto. These instruments, in the hands of musicians as different in temperament as Johnny Hodges, Charlie Parker, Benny Carter, and Lee Konitz, take on all the shadings of personality, all the colors of mood and moment of the human voice itself. Far more than the clarinet, the saxophones have made the individual known in jazz for what he is or isn't, capricious or carping, sorrowful or somnolent, sweet or sour, dashing or determined or most artfully withdrawn.

Composers in the classical symphonic tradition have been notably unsuccessful in their employment of the saxophone. Attempts to use the saxophone in this idiom have been downright embarrassing, for reasons not altogether easy to understand until you have heard a great deal of jazz. The saxophone is an instrument for improvisation, not for predetermined performance in which the cool precision of such woodwinds as the clarinet or the oboe may be desired.

NEW REEDS

It is pleasant to be able to add the fact, at this point in the history of jazz, that there is today no reed instrument, from the clucking bass clarinet to the rasping bassoon, from the fluttering flute to the throaty English horn, which cannot be heard in this music at some time or another. Off and on, the bass clarinet, which looks a little like a soprano sax and climbs to a point an octave lower than the E-flat clarinet, has made its appearance in jazz, most successfully, perhaps, in the Duke Ellington band. In the 1950s, the flute, especially as played by Herbie Mann, Sam Most, and Frank Wess, established a place for itself as a solo instrument in chamber jazz of high tension but not too many decibels.

NEW BRASS

A variety of brass instruments can now be said to be a regular part of jazz. The bass trumpet and the valve trombone, essentially interchangeable instruments, have from time to time deepened the brass texture of the post-World War II big band. The French horn has been an important part of the recent experimental writing in jazz, making an important contribution to the most significant of Miles Davis' recordings in the middle forties and in the playing of John Graas adding much to a large number of West Coast dates. Even the great-souled blasts of the tuba family have emerged again in modern jazz, now as part of the Claude Thornhill orchestra, again in the Miles Davis ensemble, even once or twice in solo performances at jazz concerts.

ACCORDION

A similar refusal to say no to any instrument has brought the accordion from Coventry, so to speak, or perhaps one should say from distant Shep-Fields, to a place of respect, as played by musicians like Mat Mathews. For Mat and one or two others have demonstrated that this reed instrument outfitted with a keyboard could be so altered as to make a thoroughly swinging and remarkably fleet jazz vehicle. While the accordion has not contributed to jazz quite the percussive blendings of the xylophone and vibraphone, it has a place, really, side by side with those great rows of blocks associated with musicians like Red Norvo, Lionel Hampton, Terry Gibbs, and Teddy Charles.

XYLOPHONE AND VIBRAPHONE

The xylophone consists of graduated bars of hard wood; the vibraphone or vibraharp of metal bars, with resonating chambers beneath each one, amplified electrically. Both, of course, are struck with mallets to make their distinctive sounds, the electronic instrument now much more a part of jazz than the xylophone, which in the wrong hands sounds like little more than the marimba's big brother.

PIANO

Like the vibes, the piano is at once a percussion instrument and a solo melodic voice in jazz, today much more the latter than the former. For years consigned in the big jazz band to a rhythm-section role, with the advent of a jazz in which no rhythm instrument is entirely without its own line, its own melodic temperament, the piano has achieved in jazz a stature just short of its role in the classical concert hall. And for all practical purposes, too, the techniques of modern jazz pianists are indistinguishable from their conservatory-trained counterparts, largely, perhaps, because so many of them have had a similar schooling. It is true, however, that many jazz pianists still flatten and stiffen their fingers more than the classically trained keyboard artists and that they will, some of the time, still sacrifice a delicacy of sound to the persuasive percussive power of the pianoforte, inflected more *forte* than *piano*.

ORGAN

Only a few hardy jazz pianists, such as Fats Waller and Count Basie, have attempted to swing the great console of the pipe organ into line, but the electronic version of the instrument has become a fixture in jazz. Its ebullient humors are particularly effective behind a modern-day blues singer; its substantial range, which varies from manufacturer to manufacturer, extends sufficiently beyond that of the piano to permit such an artist as Jimmy Smith to raise whole tiers of sound, making the organ the orchestral instrument it was always intended to be by such composers as Johann Sebastian Bach.

STRINGS

If the organ, why not the violin, the viola, the cello? Well, all three have been at various times a part of jazz, the viola and cello really not much more than teammates of reeds or substitutes for clarinet or saxophone. Stuff Smith, in the thirties, showed what brilliant, endlessly imaginative use could be made of the fiddle, if a sufficient disregard for precise intonation and an efficient attack, almost savage in intensity, could be regularly combined. In later years the more formally fashioned talents of Paul Nero have moved sometimes easily, sometimes uneasily, in jazz, always suggesting at the very least that the violin has a present if not a future in jazz. The difficulty would seem to be that of any instrument so fiendishly difficult to execute accurately that improvising must remove any performance on it far from the proprieties of pitch: as long as one trains string instrumentalists to a fastidiousness of performance, there will not be much room for them in a jazz band, where it is possible to play a trumpet or a tenor saxophone, a trombone or a piano or an organ with great precision and still produce any savagery of tone or great rhythmic outburst that may be demanded by any kind of playing occasion.

DRUMS

Last of the groups of instruments in jazz is of course the great corps of drums. What an enormous change has been effected in drums and drumming since New Orleans marching days! Originally, under the impulse of syncopated accents, regular rows of weak and strong beats, the bass drums, the snares, and the cymbals were a simple enough, if monotonous, part of jazz. Many changes in drumming over the years have placed emphasis from time to time on pseudo-African beats made on the highly sophisticated version of jungle drums called the tom-toms; on the Afro-Cuban sound of the bongos, those small drums on which the fingers do the work of sticks; on the conga, the long Latin-American drum with the deep tone; on various gongs, large and small and medium-sized cymbals, with continuing respect for that well-clapped pair of cymbals operated by the foot called the "high-hat." The place of such percussive devices as the ass's jawbone, maracas, claves, whistles, tambourines, castanets, and the like has never been secure in jazz, but such provocative thinkers among recent jazz composers as Charlie Mingus have become convinced that nothing that was ever a part of the drummer's repertory of sound effects should be banished from jazz precincts. It is the reasoning of these musicians that since drummers, in line with the whole rhythmic development of jazz, have been made free of the need to do nothing but lay down a steady beat, and that since they have developed a linear expression of the stability of the bass and the guitar in the rhythm section, so too should they be permitted all the colors and textures available to them by skill or tradition or both.

As jazz went in its curious cycle from small band to big band to small, most of its major changes of instrumentation were effected. From the Dixieland ensemble came the essential structure of the swing band: three to five trumpets; two, three, or four trombones; four or five saxophones (usually two altos and two tenors, with a baritone making the fifth member of the enlarged section), and a rhythm section consisting of piano, guitar, bass, and drums. With the advent of bop, and later of cool jazz and that variety of modern categories for which no precise name can be found, every sort of instrumentation become acceptable in jazz, with a certain conventional acceptance of a smaller rhythm section consisting of piano, bass, and drums, and a front line of trumpet, alto and/or trombone or tenor. To this basic group the experimenting modernist will add any instrument that comes along well commanded and commended by its performer—organ or accordion, flute or oboe. A certain number of groups have foregone the great orchestral reach of the piano or any other keyboard instrument in order to emphasize the austere elegances of baritone sax and trumpet, as in the case of Gerry Mulligan, or have experimented with at least certain fixed numbers of measures without drums or any other rhythm accompaniment or support. Today there is no stated or unstated limitation to the possible number of combinations of instruments in jazz, or to the kinds of sound instruments can make, the kinds of music that this or that combination of instruments can or should produce.

The one great change in the playing of jazz in the last fifteen years, one that has been made quite consciously, has been toward a more and more "classical" sound. Less and less has the vibrato associated with such a tenor saxophonist as Coleman Hawkins or such an alto man as Johnny Hodges been characteristic of jazz reed playing. More and more have brass instruments tended to sound like demurely inflected saxophones, in imitation sometimes felicitous, sometimes most unbecoming, of the playing of Lester Young on tenor or the playing of Charlie Parker on alto. Whatever the future for these procedures may be, it is clear that the jazzman has become so resolute in his pursuit of absolute control over every possible resource of his instrument, every technical facet of his horn, that he may conceivably have lost some of his concern for color, but not that general mastery which as long ago as 1926 made it possible for John Redfield, in writing a book about *Music as a Science and an Art* (Knopf, 1926), to pay the following tribute to the instrumental command of jazzmen:

There is probably no wind instrument in a jazz orchestra that is not better played by jazz artists than by symphonic musicians. It would be indiscreet to disclose how great is the percentage of symphonic musicians who would willingly desert the symphony for jazz if they were able to meet the technical requirements of the latter organization.

3 the schools of jazz

All jazz is divided into schools, to which jazzmen show a fierce loyalty. Whether members of the faculty, student body, or alumni, they have a phenomenal attachment to their old and new colleagues, the playing procedures they developed together, and everything, substantial and accidental, in any way associated with their schools.

These are real institutions; though they possess no campus sites, the sentiments stirred by them are real and quite deserved. For from the geographical locales of the founding schools of jazz and one or two of the modern schools, and from the personalities who developed the other groups of styles and stylists, have come the impetus and inspiration for the growth of jazz. At the lowest moments in jazz history, when no future seemed better than dismal, new schools have sprung up with the alertness of a fox, the endurance of a whale, and all the resourcefulness which is the birthright of jazz. With this in mind one can forgive some of the excesses of emotion, the distortions of fact, the errors of fancy with which the fondness of jazzmen for their schools is expressed. And even if for the rest of us, more or less on the outside, these exaggerations are so easily identifiable as such, they really can be marked up to the credit of the human spirit—the human spirit which is as much a part of jazz as it is of any other art, or of any other sizable undertaking of a related kind.

NEW ORLEANS

Take Storyville, for example. Much is unpleasant about this notorious red-light district in New Orleans where musicians gathered together the sounds and styles and influences that became jazz. Not for all the humor and bright color of anecdote; not for all the lusty private history and public chronicle; not for all the *argot* and the cuisine of the French Quarter—not for any of these things, no matter what their intrinsic delights, can the ugly facts of a sleazy existence be effaced or forgotten. This was gutter life, this life of the barrelhouse and brothel, and no romanticizing can do anything to lift it far above the level of the sewer. But this, nonetheless, is where jazz emerged; this for those who first played it, when "it" was first given a name, was home.

The basic structure of a jazz school was created by the first New Orleans or Dixieland musicians. From Storyville and environs came a way of combining instruments, of setting trumpet lead and collateral solos and ensembles, of creating out of a catch-as-catch-can wrestling match the outlines of a musical art. So persuasive was this procedure that for all too many it still represents the only possible approach to jazz. As a matter of fact, it is not enough to call it an "approach," because in the New Orleans school a pattern is kept, from opening notes to final rideout, which has come to be known as Dixieland, a schema so rigidly enforced by those who are convinced that this is "the real jazz" that any deviation from it, in instrument or order of solos or chord structure or voicing, is regarded as a major heresy. Out of surroundings remarkably impure has come the purist jazz school, an all too self-righteous, smug, and intolerant institution.

If one joins too easily in the fervent antiquarianism of the New Orleans school, one misses perhaps the whole substance of jazz, the vast development of this music from a bawdy-house background to an art form of large resources. On the other hand, if one turns one's back on it altogether, out of disgust at making the extrinsic so important and at excluding musicianly standards in the judging of jazz, one also runs the risk of missing a great deal. For from New Orleans came not only the drive that led jazz up the Mississippi River and out, in radiating tributaries, across the plains and mountains to both coasts and around the world, but a certain wit and wisdom too, and performers to establish both. There is a crude but essentially sound humor in the solo and ensemble exchanges of the early bands, which, when they do not become consecrated and, as a result, inflexible, make for bright beginnings for delightful solos. There is a crackling charm about what we have on record of these first performers which should never have been forgotten in fact, as it has never been forgotten in principle, in the best of jazz. This charm is a sort of irony, a scorn of the sentimental, a skepticism in the face of emotional extravagances, which, however rudimentary in form in New Orleans or Dixieland jazz, is the same kind of wise and witty thinking, the same sort of scorn for the pompous, which is to be found in swing or bop or cool jazz.

Surely, then, we should honor any of the survivors of this period who are still to be heard, whether as feeble performers or old men reminiscing, truly or fancifully, about their colorful past. And while we must continue resolutely to research the background of jazz, pulling up roots into the light wherever we find them, exhausting the achives of that eighteenth- and nineteenth-century American culture which gave background, if not birth, to this music, we must not confuse a broad general setting, hazy at best, with a thoroughly clear foreground, a landscape alive with figures, each one of whom is distinct to the eye and ear.

CHICAGO

For a long time those of us who have written about the history of jazz have contentedly accepted the fact of a Chicago jazz, a music that succeeded the first sounds of New Orleans and drew to new precincts essentially new sounds. It is clear today, however, now that a sufficient perspective has been achieved, that the musicians who settled in Chicago in the great years for jazz, from the beginning of World War I to the time of the 1929 depression, were simply New Orleans jazzmen growing up, or were their disciples and devotees. For the major figures of Chicago jazz are, with few exceptions, men like King Oliver and Louis Armstrong, who came from the Crescent City, and the members of such bands as the Louisiana Five, the Original Dixieland Band, the New Orleans Rhythm Kings. The youngsters at Austin High and their friends, those who did originate and develop in and around Chicago, were thoroughly indebted to the New Orleans émigrés for almost all their jazz ideology.

One cannot help feeling affection, and indeed respect, for the clarinet playing of Frank Teschemacher; Bix Beiderbecke's achievement is unmistakable; the playing together of men like Muggsy Spanier, Jess Stacy, Bud Freeman, Jimmy McPartland, Dave Tough, Joe Sullivan, Eddie Condon, and all the others who worked so enthusiastically together in the twenties, is continuing testament to the vitality of the jazz that had come north as much as it is to the talents of these men. One denies nothing to the Chicagoans if one credits the enormous impact of the Dixieland they first heard and then imitated and gave such additional power.

Certainly, as a convenience in cataloging recording dates and club engagements, the construction of a "Chicago period" in jazz is to be encouraged. Certainly one can blame nobody who enjoys the time-honored occupations of making lists, or gathering together the scrappy mementos that may remain of public and private buildings, restaurants and night clubs, every sort of Chicago landmark. Chicago can supply the makers of jazz scrapbooks with every sort of satisfaction as a hunting ground, providing, as it does in quantity, tattered programs, soiled menus, brown or gray or green photographs—just the sort of trivia that can summon up, irresistibly, the remembrance of things past.

NEW YORK

It is hard to find anything like a clear jazz style that we can associate with New York. Nonetheless, in the 1920s the development of big-band jazz may be said to have been essentially the work of musicians in New York. It was here that Fletcher Henderson created the band made up of swinging sections, each one conceived at once as a team of musicians making a concerted sound together, and as so many soloists who could be counted upon to make individual contributions to a jazz performance. It was in New York that Duke Ellington matured as a leader and composer and arranger, and with him all his brilliantly endowed soloists and section men. Uptown in New York, Harlem jazz was created, the very epitome of the free-swinging band, the very special incubator of the swing-era band.

The names associated with New York jazz are many: Fletcher and Duke, Don Redman and Benny Carter and Luis Russell, Chick Webb and Teddy Hill and Willie Bryant, Red Nichols and all his colleagues of short- or long-term affiliation. They have not too much in common besides the beat and the chronological position that they occupy together, somewhere between the founding fathers and the swing classicists of the thirties. But that is enough to suggest at least the rough outlines of a school and to give all these men, working together in the same place at the same time, a kind of common identity.

KANSAS CITY

Far more than Chicago or New York, the music played in Kansas City in the late twenties and early thirties may be said to have had a definable style. This is where, on both sides of the Kansas River, that bumptious music we associate with Bennie Moten and Andy Kirk and Count Basie got started. This is where a variety of small outfits led by musicians who ultimately joined one or the other of the bands mentioned—Jack Washington, Walter Page, Buck Clayton—blew such fresh, free-wheeling jazz. This is where Ben Webster and Budd Johnson grew up as musicians and made the tenor saxophone grow just a little more too. This is where Mary Lou Williams emerged as a brilliant pianist and composer and arranger. This is where the blues was converted into a most remarkable big-band music, serving equally well singers like Jimmy Rushing and Joe Turner and Walter Brown, and saxophonists like Lester Young and Charlie Parker. This is where that fluent arranging style invented by Fletcher Henderson developed another swing to its bow and the music of fourteen, fifteen, sixteen musicians demonstrated again and again all the spontaneity of four, five, or six improvising together, jumping figurations coming so easily into written or head arrangements that it all sounded, at the peak of Kansas City jazz in the mid-thirties, as if extemporized on the spot, and yet never lost the clear outlines of organized form.

The trail of Kansas City jazz leads as far as that of New Orleans does—all the way around the world. It was from the performances or the arrangements or the solos of Kansas City musicians that so much of the vitality of the swing era came. Much of the strength of bop can be traced back to Kansas City. Historically, musically, it looms larger all the time in any serious examination of the sources and resources of jazz.

SWING

With swing, the most loosely organized and least self-conscious of jazz schools, the shaping force in jazz moves from the geographical to the stylistic. With elements of Dixieland and Kansas City jazz about evenly mixed, generously seasoned with the sharp condiments of big bands out of New York and Los Angeles and many points in between, a great synthesis of all that had been in jazz until the mid-thirties was effected. A movement of Gargantuan size swept across America and changed jazz from a back-room music, associated with gangsters and prostitutes, into the classical American musical expression, as properly a part of a dignified hotel dining room as it was a legitimate attraction in Carnegie Hall or the Philadelphia Academy of Music or on a college campus.

As one listens today to the music of swing, one can hear either the accents of the past, for example, in the elegant Dixieland clarinet of Chicago musician Benny Goodman, or the massive two-beat jazz of the band of Memphis musician Jimmie Lunceford, or the unmistakable announcement of the jazz yet to come in the playing during those years of Charlie Christian and Jimmy Blanton, Roy Eldridge and Harry Edison, Dizzy Gillespie and Lester Young, Budd Johnson and Clyde Hart. And over all one must hear that great development which made such a change in the listening habits of Americans, which earned for jazz a respect that not even several years of harrowing jukebox music, during and after World War II, could wipe out; it is safe even against the monstrous caricature of this music which is "rock 'n' roll." It is for this development that one again and again returns to the jazz of the swing era to listen for the ever-expanding instrumental and scoring possibilities for old and new sounds, for musical ideas from places as far removed from the normal precincts of jazz as Vienna and Havana. And not only do listeners do this, but jazzmen also. The resolute recollection of the past which has become so firm a part of an emancipated jazz teaching, of jazz thinking, of schooled jazz playing, centers upon swing. To the musicians of that era go the jazzmen of this one, constantly refurbishing and refashioning the rhythmic and melodic patterns, the scoring and blowing procedures which have given to swing a permanent and central place in jazz.

BOP

In Chapter 1's brief history of jazz, tribute was paid to the bop school for its cultivation of tastes and techniques without which jazz might have fallen into the rut of endless self-imitation. It is sad to have to report at this point that what started as a revolt against the cliché has become too much of the time fixed in the repetition of well-worn phrases and much too well-known playing routines. The most electrifying of all of bop's contributions to jazz, its conversion of syncopated rhythmic backgrounds into exquisite cadences—fresh and original lines approaching the integrity and ingenuity of a horn blower's melodies—has very frequently been lost in a return to some of the least engaging of swing patterns, the monotonous alternation of weak and strong accents slammed onto the cymbals by the drummers and echoed naggingly by the other members of the rhythm section. But if this is true, it is also a fact that the most talented musicians of bop, or at least the best of those still alive—Dizzy Gillespie and J. J. Johnson, Bud Powell and Miles Davis, Max Roach and Kenny Clarke—remain individuals fully capable of their own ideas and sufficiently free of the narrower strictures of the school of which they are the trustees.

COOL JAZZ

The prevailing winds in the jazz of the early fifties were cool, sometimes frigid. The revolt against flag-waving arrangements and crudely defined sound of any kind took more and more the form of a restrained chamber music played on fewer and fewer instruments at any given time. Much of the best of bop was retained by these masters of understatement, those directly tied to this school, such as Stan Getz and Gerry Mulligan and Chet Baker, or those men indirectly affiliated, such as Lennie Tristano and Dave Brubeck, Lee Konitz and John LaPorta. Actually, it is difficult to think of these men today as working together in anything more than a drive to make freshness and experiment and the speculative employment of a full-fledged musicianship constantly more important in jazz. Whatever excesses they or their imitators may have been guilty of in their drive away from drive, in their pursuit of the elusive and the recondite in jazz, they did a very good turn for the music of this era in extending to all who could think on their instruments the great consolation of a contemplative approach to improvisation.

WEST COAST

Once more, in the mid-fifties, geography has become a defining factor in jazz schools. In Southern California today a number of refugees from the inclement weather and unfortuitous economy of New York (at least as far as jazz is concerned) have gathered together for jazz purposes with a few local musicians and others who have settled down around the palm trees to a steady income. They have constructed a school of jazz in which off-moments have become on-, in which time away from the radio and television and movie studios where they make their living has become the regular occasion for carefully organized playing sessions. It would be wrong to call all these affairs jam sessions; there is too much of the contrived—scores worked out with just so many measures left tacit for improvisation—to call this strictly ad lib blowing. But one way or another, these men have zealously attacked the problems involved in making jazz more free and fresh. They have attempted the writing of a jazz symphony; they have picked up every sort of mathematical device for the elaboration of musical ideas; they have examined and re-examined the possibilities of counterpoint of a classical kind for jazz and every likely transference of jazz sounds into classical forms. They are a thoughtful and provocative lot, these Coasters. They have failed to make adequate use of all the musicians available to them in that large area which gives them their name, the colored as well as the white, and their experiments have not often extended beyond the conventional three to six to ten minutes of jazz. But they have distinguished themselves for their consistent efforts to avoid the banality and the bromide, for the handsome attempt they have made to belie the ancient tradition that a jazzman who once turns to commercial music can never again blow convincing jazz.

THE NEO-CLASSICAL SCHOOL

This name, borrowed from another music, is an attempt on my part to point to the East Coast equivalent of the California school, to what is being accomplished today by musicians such as Teddy Charles, Jimmy Raney, George Russell, Teo Macero, the Modern Jazz Quartet, Charlie Mingus, and those who pass through the ateliers of Lennie Tristano, John LaPorta, and the Sandole brothers. These men have tried to effect something like a balance between the traditions of jazz and twentieth-century classical music, using materials sometimes borrowed from the twelve-tone composers, sometimes from Paul Hindemith, sometimes from a much earlier counterpoint. It is much of the time an uneasy balance, maybe even an imbalance; it differs from student to student and experiment to experiment; it is unfair to saddle all these men with the same approach, the same aim, the same achievement or lack of one. It is clear, however, that some exchange between the two kinds of music is possible, though perhaps the identifying characteristics of jazz will be lost unless, as in the playing of a Charlie Mingus, a Bernard Peiffer, a Jimmy Smith, or a Lennie Tristano, the emphasis is sufficiently upon the beat and the improvised line to keep what develops, no matter what the classical influence, a spontaneous music, a swinging music—that is, jazz.

Detroit has for many years extended a welcoming ear to modern jazz. In the mid-forties, it was particularly receptive to such bands as Georgie Auld's and Dizzy Gillespie's. Its jazz fans were among the first to organize themselves into audiences to listen to concerts of an advanced and adventurous chamber jazz. Charlie Parker was always very welcome in Detroit and with him any and all of his associates. And now in the late fifties something like a new school, perhaps the logical successor to bop, has begun to emerge in Detroit.

The new Detroit jazz is very close to bop; but unlike most of the latter-day continuations of this music it is not restricted by a slavish reverence for every note blown by the original boppers. This school boasts several distinguished men. To begin with there is the widely talented Jones family, consisting of pianist Hank, drummer Elvin, and that most original of the younger trumpeters, Thad Jones, who is especially notable among post-bop trumpeters for the fact that what he plays is so insistently "trumpetistic." Then there are the Jackson brothers, the able bassist Alvin, and that master of the long and artfully constructed vibraphone line, Milton. The trumpeter Donald Byrd gives every evidence of developing a personality of his own, in spite of his obvious indebtedness to Dizzy Gillespie and Miles Davis and Clifford Brown. Bernard McKinney has turned the euphonium into a modern jazz instrument without losing any of the essential sweetness of his horn. A similar quality informs the playing of the tenor saxophonist Yusef Lateef, one of the veterans of modern jazz to join up with the youngsters in Detroit. Finally, in this group which provides not

only soloists in quantity but rhythm sections at least two
men deep on each of the instruments, there is the remarkably
facile pianist Barry Harris.

THE SCHOOLS OF CRITICISM

A last word for schools even more conscious of themselves
and all that gives them their special place in jazz than the
musicians: the critics. From time to time something like
violence has erupted in jazz as defenders of Dixieland have
thrown themselves headlong (and not always figuratively)
at offenders from the camps of swing or bop, cool jazz or
still more modern music. The compliment and the cudgels
have been returned by those resolved to keep jazz "progressive," pushing ahead, up to date—next year's date or that
of the year after. One can regret some of the blood that
has been spilled; one can counsel, with hindsight or fore-
sight, more moderation of judgment. But moderation in
jazz has often meant mediocrity, and the very violence of
these conflicts has bred a candor which has opened the way
to progress of many kinds, clear progress at least in the continuing expansion of the serious and knowing jazz audience,
the audience for all kinds of jazz, the audience which has
drawn this music more and more out of the club into the
concert hall and the classroom.

There was a time when the adherents of the ancient and
the pristine in jazz, the do-or-die Dixielanders, were determined to assert the purity of their music. Sneeringly, they
went at all else in jazz as a shocking compromise with the
devil, a toadying to the public and the power elite that looms
so terrifyingly in the music industry. That is changed today.

Most of the apologists for Dixieland have developed—at least so far as their public utterances are concerned—a taste for bop, for Charlie Parker, and a few other moderns. Their struggle is now centered not on the attempt to isolate the early jazz from the debased music that followed it, but on pushing the music farther and farther back in time until it shall have landed squarely on its beat in the West African jungle. To this writer the results of such conjecture have been anthropologically dubious at best and rarely of much value in developing the story of jazz. There is the questionable by-product, too, of the association of jazz with primitive people making primitive sounds for primitive purposes. Whether the results are Jim Crow or Crow Jim: whether one believes that jazz can be played effectively only by white men or only by Negroes, the effect is to turn jazz into the quaint folk expression of a species of charming but essentially backward people. This is all the more uncomfortable because it sorts so poorly with the facts of the music, which simply will not resemble in its essentials the music of Africa.

Present-day jazz critics are not members of a school so often as their precursors were. There are broad divisions that remain, separating the Africanists and the purists from those, such as this writer, who feel that jazz did not develop its identifying qualities until after the turn of the century, from those who look forward rather than backward for substantial accomplishment in this music. There are a number of articulate reviewers and critics who take up and put down whole sets of critical terms and attitudes with each style they have to judge or describe, almost as if they had interchangeable ears with which to listen to a barrelhouse pianist or a bopper, a Chicago band of the late twenties or a California one of the mid-fifties. This is effective as long as it merely stresses the distinctions between one kind of music and another in the history of jazz; it is suspect for some of us when it insists that the critical evaluation of an art as young as this one cannot be achieved without a half-dozen or more sets of values—even, if necessary, conflicting values.

The end result of this attitude, it seems to me, defeats the very purpose for which ostensibly it was set up: to insist upon the existence of long lines of tradition that connect all the different parts of jazz to each other. For what these critics do is assemble a poorly assorted set of fragments, which makes jazz seem little more than a game of musical chance in which the pieces can be brought together only haphazardly rather than an integrated expression in which order and purpose can be found and described—that is, an art.

4 the elements of jazz

The definition of jazz has always been surrounded with mystery. Some of those who write or talk about it, even a few who play it, have deliberately insisted upon the enigmatic nature of jazz and have refused even to examine the possibility of analysis. Others, after examining the music in some detail, have confessed themselves baffled by elements so difficult to define and have insisted that there was something beyond the merely melodic or harmonic or rhythmic that simply was not susceptible of verbal definition. The strong impression remains, after an examination of both approaches to jazz, that in its essential nature there is a mystery unlike that of any other art.

Just how true is this? Is it any more true of jazz than it is of music in general, or painting or sculpture or poetry? Is it possible really to define with any certainty the substance, the essence, of any art? Is the definition not, rather, in the doing? Do we not really identify poetry by the performance of poets and thus content ourselves that we can recognize the phenomenon even if we cannot altogether effectively define it? And should we not really be at ease with a comparatively simple phenomenological definition of jazz?

To the extent that a series of questions, no matter how rhetorical, suggests mystery, then a mystery jazz will remain after this chapter has been read. But if one is sensitive to the forms of any art and the content thus expressed, one may find satisfaction here in a brief examination of the phenomena of jazz—the defining phenomena which produce in some the phenomenon we call jazz.

Jazz obviously is a form of Western music. For all the efforts of some to root it elsewhere, it clearly finds its background, materials, and habits of being and becoming in the European melodic, harmonic, and rhythmic traditions. If one listens to jazz, one must surely recognize that it is diatonic: that is, its melodies and harmonies are, like the rest of Western music, based upon whole tones and half tones arranged in octaves. For an understanding of what distinguishes the melodic and harmonic substance of jazz, one must go to the origins and development of Western music; the relationships that distinguish our tonalities from those of the East are no more particular to jazz than they are to the music of Beethoven or Victor Herbert, John Philip Sousa or Johann Sebastian Bach.

Jazz has made some alterations in the melodic traditions of the West. It sometimes seems to approach the subtleties of pitch, the quarter tones and microtones of Eastern music and some Western imitations of it, in its motion toward or away from a particular note. These inflections are unmistakably clear in singing such as Billie Holiday's and in the performance by Johnny Hodges or Rex Stewart on such instruments as the saxophone and the trumpet where one can scoop pitch, bend a note, sail into or away from a particular tone from above or below it. There has always been in jazz, too, a restlessness with the key concept, as the blues indicates in its acceptance all at once of the flatted third and seventh, which are the blue notes of the scale, and the natural inflections of those notes as notes in the same key. This, of course, is not strictly speaking a jazz phenomenon; a large-scale development away from fixed tonality has marked the work of many in European music in our time, from Debussy's first whole-tone writing through the polytonal composers to the twelve-tone school of Schönberg and Webern and Berg and their descendants and disciples.

Harmonically jazz has moved in a remarkably short time— less than half a century—from the simplest sort of chord structure to the most complex. It has achieved its present harmonic breadth through augmenting and diminishing and inversion, through alterations of a serious kind and of the most frivolous—the merely ornamental. Jazz harmonies have in recent years reached the point where little that can be achieved in the superimposition of sound upon sound is foreign to jazz.

It is significant that the brief history of jazz in this century is characterized by a parabolic descent and ascent in which the music has first been emphatically melodic and horizontal, then harmonic and vertical, then once again emphatically horizontal. It has matched, in this not always graceful arc, the recent history of classical music, coming finally to something like a rest in our own time in long melodic lines in which music of an additive nature, played with a most captivating forward motion, has been the concern of the most advanced and influential jazzmen.

Structurally jazz has suffered over the years from the most symmetrical of concepts. It has been restricted, again as so much other Western music has, to multiples of two and four and eight, to conventionally balanced melodic statements in which a monotonous parade of figurations of two and four and occasionally eight measures has made its way into the boxlike twelve-bar or sixteen-bar or thirty-two-bar choruses of popular music. The limitation has been the limitation of popular music with its assiduous concern for the true and tried, its standards those of the box office, fixed firmly in the hackneyed and the obvious. Today there are signs of a reorganization of form, a considerable revolt against these restrictions, in the work of such musicians as Lennie Tristano and Charlie Mingus, Teddy Charles, George Russell, and the Sandoles, of Jimmy Giuffre and Teo Macero. One can look forward to a time when jazz will not be limited by empty symmetries and foolish orthodoxies of chorus length or fixed chord structure.

The need has been to hold on to certain defining limits, those which made collective improvisation possible. This has accounted for the dependence upon tunes and chords borrowed from popular music, the tidy little figures, the clearly defined choruses. Thus, in a simpler era, was it possible for musicians to get together and to stay together in performances spontaneous in certain respects at least, no matter how restricted in others.

In all this, that musical element with which the jazz musician identified himself most characteristically was the rhythm. In spite of the fact that he played, almost always in four-four time, a music that was for many years relentlessly syncopated—in spite of every sort of rhythmic circumscription, jazz made rhythmic progress, for these boundaries did not and do not really enclose jazz rhythm. This is where the mystery occurs, turning jazz away from the familiar and the obvious, giving new textures and shapes to the music to fit all the different kinds of personality that have found expression in it.

Even when it has been most monotonous, its syncopated periods falling into the most even rows of weak and strong beats, it has been impossible accurately to notate jazz rhythm. Here, in exhilarating variations of the most subtle kind, shifts of emphasis gave even the familiar dotted eighth and sixteenth notes of an earlier jazz a pleasing tension. Here the vitality of jazz asserted itself. This is the pulse, this is the drive; this is the reason why almost nothing in jazz compliments a musician so much as the adjective "swinging."

It is really impossible to reduce this mystery to note-paper description. It is generally true, as Willi Appel says in the *Harvard Dictionary of Music*, that "It would be a hopeless task to search for a definition of rhythm which would prove acceptable even to a small minority of musicians and writers on music." How much more difficult to define rhythm in jazz, where words and notes fail to do more than faintly suggest meanings and procedures. And each year the task grows more difficult because the rhythms become more complicated. Though four quarter-notes to the bar remains its common time, jazz looks beyond this nowadays to more complicated rhythms, to setting time against time in a counterpoint of rhythms, even to the sort of measureless beat which has an unmistakable pulse but cannot be reduced to a lowest common denominator.

Happily, for all the difficulties involved in running to earth jazz rhythms or any of the other formal elements of the music, one can say enough about it to make some sort of assessment of its nature possible. One can begin with the sort of definition I offered in my *History of Jazz* some years ago:

. . . it is a new music of a certain distinct rhythmic and melodic character, one that constantly involves improvisation—of a minor sort in adjusting accents and phrases of the tune at hand, of a major sort in creating music extemporaneously, on the spot. In the course of creating jazz, a melody or its underlying chords may be altered. The rhythmic valuations of notes may be lengthened or shortened according to a regular scheme, syncopated or not, or there may be no consistent pattern of rhythmic variations so long as a steady beat remains implicit or explicit. The beat is usually four quarter-notes to the bar, serving as a solid rhythmic base for the improvisation of soloists or groups playing eight or twelve measures, or some multiple or dividend thereof.

These things are the means. The ends are the ends of all art, the expression of the universal and the particular, the specific and the indirect and the intangible. In its short history, jazz has generally been restricted to short forms and it has often been directed toward the ephemeral and the trivial, but so too has it looked toward the lasting perception and the meaningful conclusion. Much of the time jazz musicians have sought and obtained an unashamed aphrodisiac effect; they have also worshiped in their music, variously devout before the one God and the unnamed gods. Like poets and painters, they are of all faiths, their doctrines are many; but they are united in one conviction, that they have found a creative form for themselves, for their time, for their place.

From this preliminary definition one can go on to a summation of form and content in jazz. These materials do group themselves into something like a recognizable pattern, making up what seems to me a satisfactory five-fold description, if not definition, of jazz.

IMPROVISATION

Nothing can be said to be jazz that is not in some way spontaneous, that is not in some manner improvised. It may be as little as on-the-spot manipulations of note valuation, changes of rhythmic emphasis, the faintest distortions of tone, the lightest tints or shades of color added or subtracted. It may be an entirely improvised performance, in which well-known tunes are developed in the traditional form we call "variations upon a theme." It may involve an entire alteration of the chord structure of a tune or the creation on the spot of a progression, of a new tune, or of no recognizable tune at all. It may be made up of great cadenza swoops or brief sweeps away from fixed time or tune or tone. As long as some element of the extemporaneous is involved, this central part of jazz, the core of the music, will have been preserved.

THE BEAT

The faith of the jazz musician of whatever school or musical conviction remains the beat: it don't mean a thing if it ain't got that swing. This is the propelling force that drives a solo forward, that makes one man's work contagious to another and moves everybody equally to that collective tension that produces rhythmic excitement and fresh improvisation. With the beat, continuity is effected in jazz. The rhythm section may be restricted to a monotonous "chunk-chunk" or "chug-chug," "plunk-plunk" or "plink-plank," or it may be free to develop its own melodic lines as it goes; the beat may be weak, strong, weak, strong, or vice versa, or the resolute one, one, one, one of bop. The beat may be packed into finite squares or strung forward in what seems like an infinite series reaching far beyond the actual limits of the performance. Those who play jazz and those who follow it closely as listeners will recognize it when it occurs; they all know that without the beat, without this pulse, music cannot be called jazz.

COLOR

Jazz is no longer dependent upon the trumpet and trombone growls effected by mutes or plumber's plungers, or both; it no longer needs the glissandos of clarinets and scoops of saxophones to produce its identifying colors. But that freedom with which musicians like Louis Armstrong and Duke Ellington's brassmen duplicated almost any sound still exists in jazz. The colors are more subtle now, expressed through more legitimate employment of reed instruments that do not vibrate half so much as they once did, by brass instruments much cooler in tone than they used to be in jazz, by a flock of instruments new to jazz—flute and English horn and oboe, bassoon and French horn and tuba—and by the organ, piped or pushed by electrons, and all the string instruments. The distortions of conventional playing procedures are fewer today, but color remains vital to jazz, for it is in the twist or turn in the blowing or fingering of an instrument, the extension or the cutting short of a note, the gasp or grasp at a sound that nobody has ever heard before in any music, that jazzmen can express all those states of being, subtle or obvious, with which their music has thus far been concerned, can express them as composer or arranger or improvising instrumentalist, or as that eighth wonder of the world who is all three.

ENTHUSIASM

This is another basic ingredient. The enthusiasm of a jazz musician is like that of a Southern political stump speaker, with much of the folklore, the secret store of information, the built-in *argot* of the down-home character talking up his work, his worries, and his sources of good cheer. This is not the artificial enthusiasm engendered by a stimulant, but the real thing elicited by the *materia prima*—jazz hot, jazz cool, or jazz lukewarm. In their music, as in their speech, jazz musicians continually take busman's holidays: they talk shop. They talk in their music, very much of the time, about their music. For many of them there is nothing else to talk about. After all, these men are still among the first generations working at the construction of an art form. This is something new and something good taking shape right before their eyes and ears. One can understand their being enthusiastic; one can better understand their music as a result of their contagious enthusiasm.

IRONY

Most of the time jazz musicians have had to work in the dark, in the slums, underprivileged or underrated, little appreciated or downright contemned. Such an atmosphere builds suspicion, hostility, or at the very least a kind of bad- or good-humored irony. Fortunately for us, it is good-humored in modern jazz, as it has been most of the time in jazz from the very beginning. It is a little bitter at the edges occasionally, like an ancient brandy of great good taste, but it is essentially sweet and full-bodied humor. Everything in the history of jazz bespeaks a healthy skepticism, a brilliant irony expressed in parody and caricature, in a splendid refusal to take seriously the sentimental extravagances of popular songs, of popular culture. One can point, for example, to the performances of the late Fats Waller, who regularly stuck out his not inconsiderable tongue at every sticky bit of nonsense that came his way. The present-day ironists dig away a little more subtly at the foolishness of the popular music and related culture of their day—a little more subtly than their predecessors but no less cuttingly. If one joins to this sort of ridicule and mockery the stoicism of Bessie Smith and the early blues singers, talking and singing about catastrophe, then one may be able to point to the most significant sort of content in jazz. This irony, this stoicism, fights pretense, takes pompousness down a couple of pegs, and usually manages to remain entertaining, engaging. No matter how hard it is to identify in a musical performance, it is an essential part of jazz, perhaps the very substance upon which the music and our interest in it survive.

5 a five-inch shelf of jazz history

It is altogether possible to gather the substance of the history of jazz on record into a five-inch shelf. The use of the word "substance" is quite literal: the essential nature of jazz is preserved in the thirty-seven long-playing records that add up to five inches of shelf space. Obviously, much is missing in the following list: the ornamental details so entrancing to those who follow jazz closely; the complex development of schools, and the growth, simple or complicated, of the styles of the larger talents; the fashioning, bit by bit, of a continuity which, from the point of view of many years afterward, seems an inescapable part of jazz. For all these limitations, however, this is what jazz is all about, these are the major figures in some of their finest moments on records. And happily, too, the chronology of jazz is not missing in this five-inch collection: the big moments of the big men are here; so are the heaviest lines, the brightest colors, the most vital textures.

A fair suggestion of the sound of the first jazz bands can be drawn from the Original Dixieland collation, the Jelly Roll Morton narration, and the superb four-volume anthology of the essential Louis Armstrong, the Louis without whom jazz would have been a lot longer climbing from the valleys to the mountains. There is enough of Bessie Smith and Bix Beiderbecke and Duke Ellington, of the pianists who shaped keyboard styles, of the bands that defined swing and the musicians and singers who extended it far beyond its original limits, to make a compiler of the following list quite content with his selection. What is missing is some of Chicago and more of New York jazz in the 1920s and the most significant big band of the formative years, the Fletcher Henderson organization, without which a modern big band arrangement would be a great deal less malleable and moving. If one sought to supplement this list with another three or four LPs, my suggestions would include Fletcher Henderson's Connie's Inn Orchestra (10″ LP Label "X" LVA-3031), which captures some of the flavor of this band, or the Harlem Jazz, 1930 set (10″ Brunswick BL58024), in which two typical sides by Fletcher Henderson's band are combined with equally characteristic performances by the Don Redman, Duke Ellington, and Luis Russell orchestras. The next might be a Red Nichols volume, any of the three on Brunswick or those on Jump, Paramount, or Riverside; Red and his various date bands, as indicated in Chapter 1, took excellent advantage of the white musicians to be found in New York in the late twenties, and under the leadership of a Beiderbecke-like cornet sound produced some neatly scored and performed sides.

These albums would help to fill such gaps as may remain in the simplified history of jazz which this collection represents. It cannot be said that the level maintained in any of these supplementary albums is as high, for historical or musical reasons, as that of the basic list. One would be wiser, if restless with it, to move on to a much longer list, a much fatter fistful of vinyl. For after the leading figures come a vast variety of musicians, closer to the average; not pygmies, but those who have not done so much so well for jazz as the giants; those who are not indispensable to an understanding of where jazz came from and where it is going and how. To go on from this group is to move into the ranks of the enthusiast, the amateur, the fanatic. The following chapter suggests next steps, large numbers of them, on the road to lingering specialization and lavish collections.

THE ORIGINAL DIXIELAND JASS BAND. 10" "X" LX3007. The most famous sides ("Tiger Rag," "Sensation Rag," "Clarinet Marmalade," etc.) made by the first of the jazz bands to reach records. These sides, recorded in 1917 and 1918, offer a fair introduction to the sound of jazz in its cradle days in New Orleans.

JELLY ROLL MORTON: *Jazz Started in New Orleans.* 12" Circle 14001. A reconstruction, part fancy and part fact, by one of the founding fathers who sometimes exaggerated his own importance in jazz but preserved much of the early atmosphere in his spoken narrative and his piano illustrations.

LOUIS ARMSTRONG: *The Louis Armstrong Story.* Four 12" Columbia ML 4383-4386. *The* indispensable introduction to jazz and to one of its greatest figures, with suitable assists and asides by Kid Ory, Earl Hines, Don Redman. Represented are the Hot Five, the Hot Seven, the great collaborations with Hines (Volume 3), and the reworkings of pop songs which made both the songs ("Body and Soul," "If I Could Be with You," "I'm Confessin'," etc.) and Louis's way of improvising upon them classical in jazz. 1925-1931.

BESSIE SMITH: *The Bessie Smith Story,* Volumes 1 and 4. Two 12" Columbia ML 4807 and 4810. The most sturdy and the most generously gifted of the blues singers, with Louis Armstrong, James P. Johnson, and Charlie Green at their best in the background. Among the masterpieces: "Down Hearted Blues," "St. Louis Blues," "You've Been a Good Ole Wagon," "Careless Love Blues" (Volume 1); "Back Water Blues," "Trombone Cholly," "Empty Bed Blues" (Volume 4). 1923-1931.

BIX BEIDERBECKE: *The Bix Beiderbecke Story,* Volumes 2 and 3. Two 12" Columbia ML 4812-4813. Bix's sweet and touching cornet in collaboration with Frankie Trumbauer and such distinguished Paul Whiteman musicians as Joe Venuti, Eddie Lang, Miff Mole, and Jimmy Dorsey in such distinguished sides as "Singin' the Blues," "I'm Comin' Virginia," "In a Mist" (Bix at the piano), and "Margie." 1927-1929.

DUKE ELLINGTON: *Ellingtonia,* Volume 1. 10" Brunswick 58002. The early masterpieces ("Rockin' in Rhythm," "Black and Tan Fantasy," "The Mooche") played by the early masters of Duke's style: Bubber Miley, Tricky Sam, Barney Bigard, Duke himself. Mostly late twenties.

DUKE ELLINGTON: *The Music of Duke Ellington.* 12" Columbia CL 558. Fine middle-period Duke, with a few older sides and thoroughly representative performances by Cootie Williams, Johnny Hodges, Lawrence Brown, Harry Carney, Ivy Anderson, etc., of the most famous Ellington tunes ("Creole Love Call," "Sophisticated Lady," "Solitude," "Caravan," etc.) 1928-1949.

DUKE ELLINGTON: *This is Duke Ellington.* 10" RCA Victor LPT-3017. The brilliant sides of the Jimmy Blanton–Ben Webster period, the early forties. "Jack the Bear," "Ko-Ko," "Harlem Air Shaft," etc.

DUKE ELLINGTON: *In a Mellotone.* 12″ RCA Victor LPM-1364. More of the superb achievement of the most imaginative and best coordinated of Ellington bands: "A Portrait of Bert Williams," "Main Stem," "I Got It Bad," "Perdido," "The Flaming Sword," "Cotton Tail," etc. 1940-1942.

EARL HINES: *Piano Solos.* 10″ "X" LVA-3023. A superb collection of 1928, 1939-40-41 improvisations (e.g., "Child of a Disordered Brain," "Body and Soul," "Rosetta") by the most influential of all the jazz pianists.

FATS WALLER. Two 12″ RCA Victor LPT-6001. A broad sampling of Fats as pianist, singer, composer, over several decades (1920s to 1940s).

ART TATUM: *The Genius of Art Tatum,* Volumes 1 and 2. Two 12″ Clef MG C-612, C-613. Handsomely recorded solos, including such Tatum classics as "Elegy," "Humoresque," "Begin the Beguine," "The Man I Love," and "Body and Soul." 1954.

COUNT BASIE: *Lester Leaps In.* 12″ Epic IN-3107. The best of 1936-1940 Basie ("Taxi War Dance," "12th Street Rag," "Dickie's Dream," the title piece), the band that best typifies the swing era, featuring Lester Young, Harry Edison, Buck Clayton, Dickie Wells, etc.

BENNY GOODMAN: *1938 Carnegie Hall Jazz Concert.* Two 12″ Columbia SL 160. *Echt* Goodman, with Jess Stacy's finest solo (in "Sing, Sing, Sing") and excellent contributions by Teddy Wilson, Lionel Hampton, Harry James, Gene Krupa, and others, in small- and large-band performances.

JIMMIE LUNCEFORD: *Lunceford Special.* 12″ Columbia ML 4804. *The* powerhouse band of the thirties and forties in some of its more adventurous scores: "Chopin's Prelude No. 7," "Uptown Blues," "What's Your Story Morning Glory," "Cheatin' on Me."

TEDDY WILSON: *With Billie Holiday.* 10″ Columbia CL 6040. Perhaps the most impressive of all the playing-singing collaborations in jazz in the standard performances of "I Wished on the Moon," "Easy Living," etc. 1935-1938.

MILDRED BAILEY: *Serenade.* 10″ Columbia CL 6094. A good introduction to one of the really sensitive jazz singers, aided and abetted by Red Norvo, Teddy Wilson, Chu Berry, Roy Eldridge, and others, in inimitable Bailey readings of "I'll Be Around," "Don't Take Your Love from Me," "Lover Come Back to Me," and the like. 1938-1940.

COLEMAN HAWKINS: *Classics in Jazz.* 10″ Capitol H-327. The best recorded of Hawk collections, showing particularly well his mixture of early and late styles and his booming tenor saxophone sound. Middle forties.

CHARLIE CHRISTIAN: *Jazz Immortal.* 10″ Esoteric ESJ-1. A remarkable on-the-spot recording by one of the men who made modern jazz and brought the guitar into its own—in an after-hours session. 1941.

CHARLIE PARKER: *The Immortal Charlie Parker,* Volume 4. 12″ Savoy MG-12014. The 1944-1948 Bird, the musician who remade modern jazz in his image—"Donna Lee," "Chasing the Bird," "Koko," and such.

CHARLIE PARKER: *Charlie Parker with Strings,* Volume 1. 10″ Clef MG C-501. Tender couplings of alto and small string orchestra, still the most successful such combination of disparate sounds made equal by the beat and a jazz musician of quality. 1950.

BUD POWELL: *The Amazing Bud Powell.* 10″ Blue Note 5003. The only pianist to translate bop altogether successfully into a jazz keyboard style, adding to the formulations of the school the product of his own fertile imagination. 1951-1953.

SARAH VAUGHAN. 10″ Columbia CL 6133. Still Sarah's most considerable achievement on records, singing such tunes as "East of the Sun" and "Come Rain or Come Shine" with such musicians of distinction as Budd Johnson, Jimmy Jones, and Bennie Green. 1950.

ELLA FITZGERALD: *Songs in a Mellow Mood.* 12″ Decca 8068. Just Ella and a pianist (Ellis Larkins) and an excellent selection of words and music of high quality, beautifully sung. 1953.

COOL AND QUIET. 10″ Capitol H-371. A neat compendium of cool jazz, a succinct sampling of Lennie Tristano, Miles Davis, and Buddy De Franco. 1949.

WOODY HERMAN: *The Three Herds.* 12″ Columbia CL 592. Ten years of modern jazz of uncommon breadth and vitality, featuring such men as Sonny Berman, Bill Harris, Shorty Rogers, Stan Getz, Ralph Burns, and Dave Tough, and such works as "Four Brothers," "Sidewalks of Cuba," "Early Autumn," and "The Good Earth." 1945-1954.

DAVE BRUBECK: *Jazz Goes to College.* 12″ Columbia CL 566. Large chunks of Dave's piano and Paul Desmond's alto recorded in campus concerts, with no record-studio restrictions. 1954.

THE MODERN JAZZ QUARTET. 10″ Prestige 160. Delicate treatments of jazz classics ("Rose of the Rio Grande") and original manuscripts ("La Ronde," "Vendome"), with just the faintest administration of Mozartean elegance and a baroque touch or two. 1953.

THAD JONES–CHARLIE MINGUS: *Jazz Collaborations,* Volume 1. 10″ Debut 17. A joyous matching of trumpet and bass ideas, with outspoken piano and drum comment too (by John Dennis and Max Roach). 1955.

6 a fifteen-inch shelf of
jazz history

The seventy-four records listed here are suggested as brothers and sisters, uncles and aunts and cousins, of the thirty-
seven named in the preceding chapter.

Here solid musical achievement, rather than chronology,
has been the concern. Wherever historical purposes are well
served by the records, there is clear identification in the accompanying comment. But by and large these sides, present-
ing soloists and singers and combinations large and small, are
offered as necessary points in the vivid graph of the central
accomplishments of jazz, and some of the more peripheral.

Records on which a number of artists are featured are
listed separately by title.

ALMEIDA, LAURINDO. *The Laurindo Almeida Quartet Featuring
Bud Shank*. 12″ Pacific Jazz PJ 1204. A nimble mixture of ac-

cents, Brazilian guitar, and California flute, demonstrating how far modern jazz can go in accommodating the apparently alien. 1954.

ARMSTRONG, LOUIS. *Louis Armstrong Plays W. C. Handy.* 12″ Columbia CL 591. Some of the best Louis A. in years in some of Handy's best: the blues named after "St. Louis," "Memphis," "Beale Street," "Aunt Hagar," and "Yellow Dog," along with "Loveless Love," "Long Gone," and similar sweetmeats. Trummy Young and Barney Bigard are the most helpful of supporters. 1954.

BASIE, COUNT. *Count Basie Swings, Joe Williams Sings.* 12″ Clef MG C 678. A solid introduction to the present-day powerhouse, with more than adequate display of the vital talents of blues and ballad singer Williams. Among those accounted for: Joe Newman, Frank Wess, Count. Among the tunes: the essential Williams piece, "Every Day," and "In the Evening," "Roll 'Em Pete," and "My Baby Upsets Me." 1955.

BEIDERBECKE, BIX. *Bix and His Gang.* 12″ Columbia ML 4811. Volume 1 of the three-volume anthology; the most free-swinging of the three, in some ways the least organized, but an indispensable part of the Beiderbecke achievement, with such sides as "Jazz Me Blues," "Royal Garden Blues," "Thou Swell," and "Since My Best Gal Turned Me Down" among the dozen represented. 1927, 1928.

BERIGAN, BUNNY. *Berigan Plays Again.* 12″ RCA Victor LPT-1003. The best known and in some ways the best of Bunny, including the classic "I Can't Get Started" and "The Prisoner's Song," the fine "Trees" and "Deed I Do." 1937, 1938.

BROWN, CLIFFORD. *Clifford Brown and Max Roach at Basin Street.* 12″ EmArcy 36070. One of the better examples of the extraordinarily finished trumpeting of Brownie, his sidekick Max, and the able outgoing tenor man Sonny Rollins. 1956.

BYRD, DONALD. *Byrd Jazz.* 12″ Transition 5. Not a masterpiece among recent LPs, but a reasonable introduction to the vibrant performing of the Detroit trumpeter and some of his talented home-town associates (among them pianist Barry Harris, tenor Yusef Lateef, euphonium player Bernard McKinney) recorded at a 1955 concert in Detroit.

CHARLES, TEDDY. *The Teddy Charles Tentet.* 12″ Atlantic 1229. An intriguing employment of vibes (Teddy) and tuba (Don Butterfield) along with more conventional jazz instrumentation in quite unorthodox scores by George Russell, Gil Evans, and others. 1956.

CROSBY, BOB. *Bob Crosby's Bob Cats.* 12″ Decca DL 8061. Swinging Dixieland of the swing era including the delightful "Big Noise from Winnetka" and some sumptuous Eddie Miller tenor ("Slow Mood" and "Can't We Be Friends"). 1937-1940.

DAVIS, MILES. *Classics in Jazz.* 10″ Capitol H 459. The unforgettable 1948 sides: "Jeru," "Godchild," "Israel," etc.

DORSEY, TOMMY. *Tribute to Dorsey,* Volume 2. 12″ RCA Victor LPM-1433. A well-chosen assortment of the less hackneyed arrangements of a variety of interesting personnels ranging from 1938 to 1946.

ELDRIDGE, ROY. *The Roy Eldridge Quintet.* Clef MG C 150. Open and muted and always moving trumpet in such standard—and delectable—Eldridge items as "Little Jazz," "Rockin' Chair," and "The Man I Love." 1954.

ELLINGTON, DUKE. *Ellington Uptown.* 12″ Columbia ML 4639. The place of honor is held by the amusing Betty Roche vocal version of "Take the 'A' Train," in which composer Billy Strayhorn plays some charming piano too. Involved too are effectively inflated performances of "The Mooche" and "Perdido." 1952.

————. *A Drum Is a Woman.* 12″ Columbia CL 951. A compact imaginative history of jazz and some related personalities, not always neatly or clearly joined together, but with sprightly episodes and often beautifully performed. 1956.

FREEMAN, BUD. *Comes Jazz.* 10″ Columbia CL 6107. One of the most successful revivals on records of Chicago jazz, with Max

Kaminsky, Jack Teagarden, and Pee Wee Russell aiding Bud in making this convincing. 1940.

GETZ, STAN. *The Stan Getz Quintet at Storyville,* Volume 1. 12″ Roost 2209. Half a dozen expansive presentations of a superb group: Stan, Jimmy Raney, Al Haig, Teddy Kotick, and the late Tiny Kahn. 1953.

GILLESPIE, DIZZY. *Dizzier and Dizzier.* 12″ RCA Victor LJM-1009. The cream of 1947-1949 big-band Gillespie, rarely sour, always tangy; including George Russell's provocative "Cubana Be, Cubana Bop," with the late Chano Pozo on bongos.

————. *Jazz Creations.* 12″ American Recording Society G-405. A variety of solid Gillespie items culled from different dates in the late forties and early fifties, including one side with strings and one with strictly Latin rhythm.

GIUFFRE, JIMMY. *Tangents in Jazz.* 12″ Capitol T 634. Fascinating experiments in rhythm by a quartet consisting of clarinet or tenor (Giuffre), trumpet, bass, and drums. 1956.

GOODMAN, BENNY. *Benny Goodman Combos.* 12″ Columbia GL 500. Benny and his most persuasive chamber-music colleagues, Cootie Williams, Count Basie, Teddy Wilson, Charlie Christian, Red Norvo, etc., in groupings of five, six, and seven. 1939-1945.

————. *Benny Goodman and his Orchestra.* 12″ Columbia GL 501. Such superior items as "Clarinet a la King," "Benny Rides Again," "Mission to Moscow," and "Clarinade." 1939-1945.

HAMILTON, CHICO. *Chico Hamilton Quintet.* 12″ Pacific Jazz PJ-1225. Cello, reeds (one or another of four), and pianoless rhythm produce a rich sound. 1956.

HAMPTON, LIONEL. *Hot Mallets.* 12″ RCA Victor LJM-1000. Some suggestion of the swinging groups Lionel used to assemble for his pick-up record sessions is contained in this collection of swing-era classics by such musicians as Cootie Williams, Johnny Hodges, Coleman Hawkins, Benny Carter, Ziggy Elman, etc. 1937-1939.

HENDERSON, FLETCHER. *Fletcher Henderson and His Connie's*

Inn Orchestra. 10″ "X" LVA-3013. Well scored, swinging 1931 jazz performed by Hawkins, Harrison, Henderson & Co.

HERMAN, WOODY. *Sequence in Jazz.* 10″ Columbia CL 6092. Ralph Burns' vertebrate large-scale opus, "Summer Sequence," and three other expert performances by the brilliant band of 1946-1947.

HOLIDAY, BILLIE. *Music for Torching.* 12″ Clef MG C 669. Billie at her latter-day best with Benny Carter, Harry Edison, Barney Kessel, and a fine rhythm section to back her up in lofty laments at various tempos. 1955.

JAZZ MESSENGERS. *The Jazz Messengers at the Café Bohemia,* Volume 1. 12″ Blue Note 1507. Kenny Dorham (trumpet), Horace Silver (piano), Doug Watkins (bass), and leader Art Blakey (drums) work over a handful of tracks with spirit and intelligence in a well-recorded night-club session.

KENTON, STAN. *Innovations in Modern Music,* Volume 1. 12″ Capitol P 189. The well-intentioned, occasionally successful attempt to merge strings and jazz instrumentation. All of it is beautifully played. 1950.

KESSEL, BARNEY. *Kessel Plays Standards.* 12″ Contemporary C 3512. Exquisite guitar playing with a small West Coast band of changing personnel in three sleek 1954 sessions.

KONITZ, LEE. *Lee Konitz with Warne Marsh.* 12″ Atlantic 1217. A moving pairing of two longtime friends and close musical associates with a superb rhythm section (Sal Mosca, Billy Bauer, Oscar Pettiford, Kenny Clarke) in support of the distinguished saxophonists. 1955.

KRUPA, GENE. *Gene Krupa and His Orchestra.* 10″ Columbia CL 6017. Some choice Roy Eldridge and Anita O'Day collaborating with a fair band in the early forties.

LaPORTA, JOHN. *John LaPorta Quintet.* 10″ Debut 10. Still the most comprehensive introduction to John's writing and playing talents. 1954.

LUNCEFORD, JIMMIE. *Jimmie Lunceford and His Orchestra.* 12″ Decca DL 8050. A substantial representation of the band when Sy Oliver was its moving spirit, seconded, of course, by Willie Smith, Joe Thomas, Trummy Young, and others. 1934-1941.

MATHEWS, MAT. *Mat Mathews Quintet.* 12″ Brunswick BL 54013. The lovely sounds of Mat's accordion, Herbie Mann's flute, and rhythm in scores worthy of them. 1953.

MINGUS, CHARLIE. *Pithecanthropus Erectus.* 12″ Atlantic 1237. A well-recorded sampling of the Mingus imagination, translated into quintet terms. This set includes the delightful adventure in San Francisco traffic Charlie made of "A Foggy Day." 1956.

MODERN JAZZ QUARTET. *Fontessa.* 12″ Atlantic 1231. John Lewis's writing stretched comfortably into ten-minute expression in the title piece; the rest of related interest. 1955.

MULLIGAN, GERRY. *Gerry Mulligan Quartet.* 12″ Pacific Jazz 1207. The pianoless group that gave modern chamber jazz such a reach up, featuring Chet Baker on the coolest of trumpets, Gerry on a baritone of similar temperature, bass, and drums. 1953.

NAVARRO, FATS. *Fats Navarro Memorial Album.* 10″ Blue Note 5004. Some of the cleanest recordings of the generously gifted bop virtuoso, trumpeter Navarro. 1948.

NICHOLS, RED. *Red Nichols Classics,* Volumes 1 and 2. 10″ Brunswick BL 58008-58009. Classics indeed, some of the most enduring of the late twenties, tunes and performers both.

NIEHAUS, LENNIE. *The Quintets and Strings.* 12″ Contemporary C 3510. One of the least imitative of modern alto men, a sensitive West Coast musician of broad tastes, whose range is excellently displayed here. 1955.

NOONE, JIMMIE. *Jimmie Noone's Apex Club Orchestra.* 10″ Brunswick BL 58006. Rich 1928 performances by the best of the New Orleans clarinetists, with Earl Hines well represented in the assisting group.

NORVO, RED. *Red Norvo Trio.* 12″ Fantasy 3-19. An attractive slice of the Norvo personality excellently sandwiched between hunks of Jimmy Raney (guitar) and Red Mitchell (bass). 1954.

OLIVER, KING. *King Oliver.* 10″ Brunswick BL 58020. The Oliver orchestra just before it passed into jazz history, with some able sidemen and enough of the trumpet-playing leader to indicate why he is held in such awe by those who heard him at his peak. 1926, 1927.

PARKER, CHARLIE. *All Star Sextet.* 12″ Roost 2210. The superb 1947 sides ("Embraceable You," "Scrapple from the Apple," etc.) made with Miles Davis, J. J. Johnson, Max Roach, Duke Jordan, and Tommy Potter.

————. *Charlie Parker.* 12″ Clef MG C 646. Some fine, fertile late Bird with a variety of musicians cast in necessarily subsidiary roles, ranging across vocal and Afro-Cuban and other devices current when the sides were made. 1951, 1953.

PEIFFER, BERNARD. *Bernie's Tunes.* 12″ EmArcy 36080. The most startling technician since Tatum, a pianist of elegance and warmth, French by birth and training, but thoroughly attuned to modern American jazz by personality and preference. 1956.

PETERSON, OSCAR. *Oscar Peterson Plays Count Basie.* 12″ Clef MG C 708. Another bravura keyboard artist handsomely provided with tunes out of the Basie library and beats out of the capacious equipment of Buddy Rich, Herb Ellis, and Ray Brown. 1956.

POLLACK, BEN. *Ben Pollack and His Orchestra.* 10″ "X" LX-3003. A fair sampling of the 1926-1929 product of the band that featured Benny Goodman, Jack Teagarden, Jimmy McPartland, and the musicians who later founded the Bob Crosby orchestra.

RAEBURN, BOYD. *Innovations by Boyd Raeburn.* 10″ Clef MG C 15012. Some of George Handy's best scores well preserved by one of the best of the early modern bands. 1946.

REINHARDT, DJANGO. *The Great Artistry of Django Reinhardt.* 10″ Clef MG C 516. Some of the late guitarist's least mannered and most moving music, most of it jazz, some of it in the modern groove. Early fifties.

SANDOLE, DENNIS AND ADOLPH. *Modern Music from Philadelphia.* 12″ Fantasy 3-209. Introduced here are two remarkable self-taught musicians, with big- and small-band playing experience, whose scores provide such musicians as John LaPorta, Teo Macero, and Sonny Russo with effective blowing points. Among the inventive flights are two of the shortest and most captivating on record, "Grenadine" and "Tamaret." 1955.

SHAW, ARTIE. *My Concerto.* 12″ RCA Victor LPT-1020. An effective collation of some of Artie's attractive experimental attempts of the early and middle forties, some fairly pretentious, but all worth rehearing.

————. *Artie Shaw and His Gramercy 5.* 10″ RCA Victor LPT-3013. The 1940 quintet featuring Johnny Guarnieri on harpsichord and the 1945 sextet with Roy Eldridge, Dodo Marmarosa, and Barney Kessel.

SMITH, BESSIE. *The Bessie Smith Story,* Volume 3. 12″ Columbia GL 505. Not only well-turned 1925-1927 Bessie Smith, but another (unrelated) Smith of rich jazz substance, trumpeter Joe, with half a dozen other excellent Fletcher Henderson musicians, among them Coleman Hawkins, Charlie Green, and Jimmy Harrison.

SMITH, JIMMY. *The Incredible Jimmy Smith.* 12″ Blue Note 1525. It is hard to choose among the three LPs that introduced Jimmy to records, but this one offers, in addition to obvious contrasts of tempo and texture, one of the wittiest of modern jazz effusions, his transformation of "I Cover the Waterfront." Easily the best equipped and most alert of jazz organists thus far. 1956.

SPANIER, MUGGSY. *Muggsy Spanier's Ragtime Band. The Great 16.* 12″ RCA Victor LPM-1295. Some of the most finely edged Dixieland of post-New Orleans days, with particularly persuasive playing by the cornetist-leader. 1939.

STITT, SONNY. *Sonny Stitt Plays Arrangements from the Pen of*

Quincy Jones. 12″ Roost 2204. A splendid natural setting for the best of the alto men to take wing from Bird. 1956.

TEAGARDEN, JACK. *Big T.* 10″ Commodore 20015. Teagarden playing and singing of high quality with able support from two sets of Nicksieland musicians. 1938, 1944.

TRISTANO, LENNIE. *Lennie Tristano.* 12″ Atlantic 1224. Five romps with Lee Konitz alternate with three masterpieces of the rhythmic and melodic imagination of this most provocative of modern jazz pianists. 1955.

WEBSTER, BEN. *The Consummate Artistry of Ben Webster.* 12″ Norgran MG N 1001. Large helpings of the large-toned, tightly organized, thoroughly relaxed tenor of the warm personality his friends call Uncle. 1954.

WILEY, LEE. *Night in Manhattan.* 10″ Columbia CL 6169. A finely balanced presentation of a jazz singer with a graceful manner and husky sound all her own. Bobby Hackett, Joe Bushkin, and strings provide taste and beat, as required. 1951.

WILLIAMS, MARY LOU. *A Keyboard History.* 12″ Concert Hall 1206. Some idea of the talents of this great lady of jazz may be gathered from this collection of pieces of three decades of jazz carefully put together here by Mary Lou at the piano, with excellent assistance from Wendell Marshall and Osie Johnson. 1955.

YOUNG, LESTER. *The President.* 12″ Norgran MG N 1005. Lots of Lester (accompanied only by rhythm), including some of his sumptuous ballad lines, among them the classical exhibition of his thinking and sounding processes, "Confessin'." Mid-fifties.

The Drum Suite. Gus Johnson, Osie Johnson, Don Lamond, Teddy Sommer; Manny Albam–Ernie Wilkins and Their Orchestra. 12″ RCA Victor LPM-1279. Subtitled "A Musical Portrait of Eight Arms from Six Angles," this exuberant employment of jazz drummers does great credit to the drummers, the leaders of the band (and composers of the *Suite*), and the recording engineers. A swinging delight from start to finish. 1956.

Giants of the Piano. Art Tatum, Erroll Garner. 12″ Roost 2213. The superb 1944 Tatum Trio sides ("Flying Home," "Dark Eyes," etc.) and some excellent 1947 Garner, notably the excellently organized "Trio" and "Pastel."

Harlem Jazz, 1930. 10″ Brunswick 58024. Just before swing in New York with Ellington, Redman, Henderson, and Russell in typical moving sides, featuring impressive soloists in impressive scores.

Kings and Queens of Boogie Woogie. 10″ Decca DL 5249. A fair assortment of the standard routines ("Yancey Special," "Pinetop's Boogie Woogie," "Honky Tonk Train Blues") and the standard performers (Ammons, Lewis, Johnson, and Cleo Brown among others). 1935-1940.

Riverside History of Classic Jazz. Five 12″ records in Riverside album SDP-11. One can quarrel about the ultimate jazz value of this or that performance made secure for posterity in this collection. One should surely challenge this use of the word "classic" to describe pre-1930 jazz. But, whatever one's appraisal of the justice of some of the choices and the language used to describe them, it is certainly good to have in one package sides—among them some excellent ones—by Ma Rainey, Bessie Smith, Jelly Roll Morton, the New Orleans Rhythm Kings, a variety of honky-tonk pianists, New Orleans and Chicago jazzmen and their followers.

A String of Swingin' Pearls. 12″ RCA Victor LPM-1373. A silly title masks some well-chosen date records of the twenties, thirties, and forties, including such classics of the period as Bud Freeman's "The Eel," the Tommy Dorsey–Fats Waller "Honeysuckle Rose," and Gene Gifford's "Nothin' But the Blues" and "New Orleans Twist." 1929-1945.

7 shelved!

The only limits to collecting jazz records are the stress and strain one's floors and fortunes can take. Several collectors have done their best to test these limits and have achieved near-bankruptcy—as well as notable collections—in the process. For some of them the switch from shellac to vinylite, from monstrously heavy as well as breakable records to the nearly indestructible microgroove platters, came just in time: the vast vibrating shelves they did accumulate were just about ready to topple into dust along with themselves, their wives, their children, and their neighbors.

Have microgroove records, wafer-thin, really solved this problem? Or have they merely put off for another decade or two that terrible point when all one's space is exhausted?

Limits there will have to be. It is no longer possible to

keep up with all the jazz of quality, even of the highest quality, that is issued each month by the eighty-odd record companies turning out significant records. In the dear dead days of swing, a month's output of the best and the second-best rarely approached as many sides as are sandwiched together in the long-playing products of only one of the big companies today. One must pick and choose among the new records and the old, if possible by principle. Otherwise the only pattern likely to be formed by one's collection is a neurotic one, the result of mad dashes from reviews and advertisements to financial ledgers and record stores, a never-ending relay race in which one always falls farther behind the disk jockeys and the presses.

This is an excellent time to look back over the past to see what out-of-print shellac records are still interesting and what LPs are not likely, because of the special nature of their contents, to be with us for very long. Obviously, any hunting of the long-playing records can be done later than the forays after the rare shellac that each day grows more rare. There is not only a constantly dwindling supply of shellac; there are fewer and fewer depots to which one can repair, such as Salvation Army piles and rummage collections and the like, and only a handful of professional outfits dedicated to the routing out of the precious remaining 78s. Very soon it may be a matter of tracking down these performances in isolated collections located at widely separated points around the world.

This is where the tape machine rears its two heads. It is wise, especially for those who are interested in the very old in jazz, to borrow and lend records for taping purposes. To these exchanges should be added all the possibilities that remain—and there are not many—of recording in person, in club or living room or recording studio, such veterans of New Orleans or Chicago jazz as may willingly subject themselves to this procedure, whether for commercial or private purposes. If one is a devotee of the most ancient playing procedures in jazz, one simply must face the fact that fewer and fewer authentic reproductions of the past can be heard today, with the exception of what is on records—all recorded after 1917—and what may be brought to new tape by intrepid explorers of the swamps and slums, the backwoods and back rooms in which the early men of jazz may still occasionally be found, occasionally still capable of playing.

It is my strong suggestion that tape become the basic tool of the serious collector of jazz who is not content to take the huge monthly releases lying down. It is possible, with the right machine, to take performances off the air by connecting tuner to amplifier, so that what comes into one's radio or television set goes directly onto tape. It is equally possible, when the proper arrangements have been made, to record privately—I repeat, privately—performances that are not going to be sold for anybody's gain but are simply going to be preserved for posterity. And with tape one can reach into any sort of collection, recombine shellac and vinylite, 78 and 45 and 33⅓ RPM tracks, make up concerts in any order that seems logical and pleasing and develop in the process a jazz collection of high individual merit, cut strictly according to personal taste.

None of this is to suggest a boycott of the many records that spill so tumultuously onto reviewers' turntables today, but simply to caution against a panicky attempt to keep up with everything new—an attempt which even a professional reviewer cannot make without seriously damaging his ears, as well as destroying a good deal of the peace and purpose of his family life. Record lists, now almost as thick as book catalogues, challenge the energy of even the super-collector with bottomless financial resources. The only strategies against the assault of records today are those of taste and learning.

Because of the records available today and the new tape machines, a whole new line of development has become possible for the record collector. Now one can start specialized collections. Now, for example, one can really put together shelves full of the best of 1935 to 1942 jazz: a cumulative documentation of swing can be had by anyone with the taste and skill and time to run down what is available on long-playing records. Today, one can keep something like an accurate record of the development of modern jazz, starting with the first sides of Charlie Christian and Lester Young and the riches of 1940 to 1943 Ellington, moving date by date through bop and the chamber music of cool jazz, and all the more recent schools. One can collect clarinetists or cornetists, trumpeters or trombonists or tenormen, male or female singers, pianists or flautists, vibists or accordionists or jugblowers, jazz quite old or very new or somewhere in-between.

There is much to be said for the special collection. Perhaps there is no better way to achieve a perspective of the whole music. As a concentration upon seventeenth-century English poets, Restoration dramatists, or modern stream-of-consciousness novelists will make more incisive one's judgment of the whole range of literature, so too will a selective approach to jazz. This may not guarantee perfect balance in one's view of jazz any more than the lover of miniatures or the ardent admirer of oversize historical paintings can expect to look at his art with absolute equilibrium. But this is a realistic way to listen to jazz, just as it is a sound approach in general to the creative intelligence as it is exercised anywhere at any time. This way one gets to know intimately some aspect—let us hope a central one—of the music; this way collecting, far from being tedious to oneself and anguishing to those around one, becomes an invitation to learning, and an indication that one has come to the heart of the matter of jazz, the creative process itself.

8 the language of jazz

There are two ways a jazz musician can be distinguished
from the ordinary run of men: by the music he plays and
by the language he speaks. It is his language that gives him
that sense of community for which he fights so hard so much
of the time. But his is more than a language; it is a kind of
code which gains him admittance to the secure circles of
jazz, establishes him as a member of an élite, and makes it
possible for him to forbid entrance to his society.

The jazz musician has every right, really, to the club life
he has founded for himself, which in its own way is as much
at a remove from ordinary society as an eighteenth-century
coffeehouse would be today. For the jazz musician has been
pushed across the tracks into what is now his own strange
world, without any thought as to whether or not that is his

natural habitat. And the jazz world is a most fertile breeding place for neologisms; its habitués are inveterate coiners of new language.

The neologisms come in quantities, to fit the needs of the jazz community. As the landscape of jazz expands, so does its vocabulary; it has become so subtle in recent years that now it is more a matter of emphasis, of accent, of the individual interpretation of individual words. But still, a certain basic terminology persists. Special words, developed out of several different kinds of slang and the imaginative resources of jazz musicians, describe with some precision a state of musical being, a wrinkle or ruffle, a twist or turn in jazz for which there is simply no known equivalent in straightforward, traditional language.

A great many of the early terms in jazz came, logically enough, from its early surroundings. The name itself cannot be run to earth with any certainty, but one of the most plausible of the many sources that have been suggested for it is the French verb *jaser,* which means to chatter, to chat, to babble, to tattle, and has an overtone which means to entertain, to make fun, to make something go faster. All these meanings attach themselves easily enough to a music played in the sporting houses of a city where some form of French was spoken for so long by the majority of the citizens. Other possible explanations of the name spring from the various "characters" who may or may not have been a part of jazz in the nineteenth century: one Charles Alexander or Charles Washington from Vicksburg, Mississippi, whose name was shortened to make *Chas* or *Chaz,* then perhaps *Jass* or *Jazz;* or one Jasbo Brown, a dancer, whose first name may have been Jasper originally; or any number of other musicians, no longer outfitted with surnames in our records, who were originally christened Charles, Jasper, Jason, or the like.

The early music was often called *barrelhouse,* after the New Orleans cabarets in which liquor was dispensed from barrels; such music was thought to be as coarse as the rude distillations with which it was associated. Another name for it was *gutbucket,* which refers to a receptacle for liquor and to music of the sort associated with such rough-and-tumble drinking. Reasonably enough, because of the occasions upon which jazz was played in the early days, an improvising session was often called a *clambake* or a *jam session,* referring to the crowds that gathered for it and the party or picnic atmosphere. And because so much of the time jazz, in the early days, was bordello or *cathouse* music, its performers were called *cats,* and by many still are. The descriptive title for that early piano blues form, *boogie woogie,* has a sexual overtone that it gets from its brothel background. And the generic term, the *blues,* may have some similar etymology, as in a *blue* story, that is, a bawdy joke.

One must be careful not to impose the stigma of early associations upon later music. It does not follow that because so much of jazz language is of dubious origin, the music itself has a questionable content, or is necessarily played with any intention related to the aphrodisiac, the suggestive. Much jazz language, similarly, has a direct underworld connection or some tie to narcotics; the relation to jazz, in these cases, is more often indirect than direct, although unquestionably the transmission from one world to another was often accomplished by pickpockets, con men, and drug addicts, who have certainly been close enough to the places where jazz has been played to make more than a casual impression upon those who play it.

But what, then, about such a word as *Schmalz,* for many years the standard jazz term for music uncomfortably sweet and treacly? This German noun, which means lard, suggests some association either with a German-speaking jazz musician, a grocer, or a butcher. Or what about those various ways a jazz musician describes that intensity of emotion connected with his music which may throw a man so far out of balance that he *blows his top,* or *snaps his cap,* or *flips his lid,* or *wigs?* The descriptive force of these expressions is clear enough; their connection with the present-day interest in psychiatry on the part of jazz musicians, as with so many others, is equally unmistakable.

One of the most important jazz words that has hung on for decades is *hip,* which once was *hep.* Some explain it as the surname of a gossip of the Chicago underworld of the 1890s; one who listened as much as he did to rumor and tattle was like him—*hep.* As jazz changed, and its language changed with it, the word to describe those who really understood jazz, the real initiates, changed from *hep* to *hip,* a familiar change in the United States, where so often *-en* becomes *-in,* so that, for example, the word *pen* is often pronounced *pin* in American dialects. Finally, the short trip from *hip* to *hipster*—a *cognoscente,* a particularly knowing musician or fan—was made.

Certain words of pejorative meaning have a clear source; others are not so easily tracked down. The word *corny,* for stale or trite or inane, unquestionably comes from *cornfed,* meaning somebody who comes from the country, a hick. The words *drag* and *bringdown,* used as verbs or nouns, refer clearly enough to a change in tempo, vitally important to jazz musicians as an index of a change in mood. The most eloquent of the jazz musician's words of contemptuous dismissal, *square* (adjective) or *a square* (noun), referring, in another venerable slang phrase, to one who is not *in the know*, one who is not *hip*, apparently has an underworld source.

Over the years a particularly important set of words have been those which describe the superlative in a jazz musician's life, something extraordinary which has happened to him or to somebody else. These words and phrases are indeed superlative: they suggest at once that high pitch of excitement to which the musician's playing or listening to another's playing may move him, and the lengths to which he will go to find some verbal equivalent for the musical and emotional experience. Thus he calls these moments *crazy* or *gone* or *the end;* thus in the early forties he spoke of being moved *out of this world;* thus, very briefly, he described an unusually moving musical experience as one which *sent* him. Today a musician who plays particularly well, who is unmistakably inspired, is *wailing* or *wails;* or, with that present-day taste for the delicate shade of meaning, a word used to describe a peak of restraint, *cool,* may also take on all the overtones of the other superlatives discussed here.

There are many other key words in jazz, new or old, outmoded or still current, which the list that follows should make abundantly clear. But no list set in type can conceivably fix once and for all any kind of specialized vocabulary, particularly one in which so much is at stake as in jazz diction. Taboos quickly fall upon words and phrases and those who use them. New kinds of jazz require new words. And then there is that endless procession of fashionable words moving in and out of the jazzman's language, the fruits, decaying or ripe, of the desire for novelty. Here the jazz musician is part of a process in slang which is not unique, at least for the United States. As long ago as 1917 this process was noted by the Yale professor of linguistics, Edgar H. Sturtevant, in his book *Linguistic Change* (University of Chicago Press):

Many new words are due to a desire for novelty. Such are the slang words which spring suddenly into popularity and for a few months seem amusing enough to enliven the dullest conversation, but which presently send a shudder down the spine of one whose slang is up to date. Not long since [in 1901] I heard a professor of my acquaintance remark jauntily, "You're off your base." That phrase was once as fresh and spicy as *have a heart* or *do one's bit* is now; but to use such antiquated slang today is equivalent to labeling yourself a *has-been*. Who wants to call his partner in the Plattsburg military trot a *lulu* or the music *hot stuff?* Yet that is what one said in the days before the schottische went out of vogue! George Ade's Artie called dollars *cases* or *simoleons*. About the year 1910 . . . the word *skiddoo* was a favorite imperative for a contemptuous dismissal.

A really accurate jazz dictionary, in addition to keeping track of verbal taboos, other changes according to fashion, and the effects upon language of developments in the music, would have to note all the variegations of speech introduced by jazz personalities. There is, for example, that vast vocabulary brought up from Louisiana by Louis Armstrong, some of it unchanged since his pre-World War I days in New Orleans, some of it shortened or lengthened to meet the needs of a letter to a Broadway gossip column, an adventure in an autobiography between book covers, or a public interview. This isn't jazz talk, necessarily, but it is a vigorous part of jazz, even as Louis is himself. There is also that interesting kind of brevity which is common to such a musician as Benny Goodman, which has led him to call everybody, from a stranger in the house to his own daughter, "Pops." And there are the little variations on verbal themes which belong to the different groups of musicians in jazz: the streams of adjectives from a dozen different sources that go with Stan Kenton's Texas and California personality; the understatement, clipped in the best British fashion, that was typical of almost all the quiet-spoken members of the Jimmie Lunceford band, as much a part of them as their soft singing or brassy but mechanically precise playing. In the same context note should be taken of that tendency to the effete, in words as well as in dress, which entered jazz with the cool era, a restraint which upon occasion became nothing less than sterile.

There is no greater danger for the newcomer to jazz, whether fan or musician, than the attempt to speak a language he does not understand. Nothing shows him so *square;* nothing makes him so immediately a *drag* to those around him. All too easily he falls for the pseudo-jazz vocabulary, for those terrifying names for musical instruments which no jazz musician in his right mind has used in decades, if anyone ever did: *bull-fiddle, dog-house, licorice stick, slush-pump,* and like horrors. No jazz musician will be irritated to hear his instrument called by its full name, as for example a baritone saxophone or a vibraphone. It is never necessary to *goof* or to *dig;* it will be enough if one apologizes for failing to make an appointment or demonstrates, in conventional language, that one follows the conversation of a jazz musician.

Understanding is the key word of the jazz musician's use of this vocabulary. It represents a point of view, one held by a closed community, but one which is surely bona fide. This is the way a jazz musician looks at things and listens to sounds. These words are more than shortcuts for the initiated, they do more than point: they describe and interpret. Experience with them over the years demonstrates again and again that some of them, at least, really communicate with freshness and accuracy what the jazz musician intends in his playing and thinking.

A JAZZ GLOSSARY

air-check: a recording of a radio or television performance.

Apple, the: New York City.

baby: term of endearment used interchangeably between the sexes or man-to-man or woman-to-woman.

ballad: a romantic popular song, usually slow or middle tempo, most often with a thirty-two-bar chorus.

barrelhouse: a rough-and-ready music (see page 101).

beat: as a noun, jazz time, the basic pulse; as an adjective, weary, exhausted.

blow: verb used to describe the playing of any jazz instrument, whether actually blown or not.

blow one's top: phrase expressing exasperation, enthusiasm, or insanity (for synonyms see *flip, wig,* below).

blue notes: the flatted third and seventh which create the blues scale and hence a blues performance.

boogie woogie: a piano blues form, which from time to time has been orchestrated.

bop: generic term for that form of modern jazz, originally known as *bebop* or *rebop,* which developed in the forties.

bounce: (now out of date) a buoyant beat; once particularly current in the phrase *businessman's bounce,* which described a monotonous two-beat played at a fast and nervous tempo for the delectation of tired businessmen and their partners.

bread: money.

break: a passage inserted in a performance while the rhythm is suspended, like a cadenza acting as a retarding element.

bridge: the third eight bars in a thirty-two-bar chorus (the B section in the A-A-B-A pattern or any other which uses an A-B alternation); also called the *release* or *channel.*

bring down: to depress; as a noun, *bringdown,* one who depresses.

bug: to bewilder or annoy.

cat: musician.

changes: chord progression.

character: one who is more or less interesting, but out of the ordinary.

chase: alternation of solos by two or more musicians.

chip: girl.

chops: lips.

clambake: earlier used honorifically to mean *jam session;* later used to denote an improvised or arranged session which doesn't come off.

clinker: bad note, or one that is *fluffed.*

combo: short for combination of musicians, a small band, varying in size from trio to "tentet."

commercial: music, musician, or musicianship designed solely for fame and fortune; also a sponsored radio program.

cool: restrained; also a superlative of broader meaning in modern jazz (see page 103).

corny: stale, trite; also *cornball,* a noun meaning one who is *corny.*

crazy: superlative, used either as adjective or interjection.

cut or *cut out:* to leave, to depart; the first also means to outdo a soloist or band in competition.

dad or *daddy-o:* an endearing form of address.

deejay: disk jockey.

dig: to understand, to penetrate with particular astuteness; also to enjoy or to affirm.

disk jockey: record announcer on radio or television.

Dixieland or *Dixie:* early jazz, especially of the New Orleans variety.

dog tune: a song of questionable musical quality.

drag: as a verb, to depress; as a noun, one who lowers another's spirits.

drive: to play with concentrated momentum.

eyes: usually the object of a verb, as in *"to have eyes,"* to be interested, to want to do something.

fake: to improvise.

fall in: to arrive.

fall out: to leave.

flip: as a verb, to lose one's head; as a noun, an original, an eccentric.

fly: smooth (to describe looks or manner of performance).

four beat: (little used today) an even four beats to the bar.

fracture: to "knock somebody out," to move, or to inspire.

funky: down-to-earth, a blues feeling, *groovy.*

gas: as a verb, to arouse, to stir feelings; as a noun, something that is stirring (also *gasser*).

gate: once upon a time synonymous with jazz musician; used as well to designate Louis Armstrong or Jack ("Big Gate") and Charlie ("Little Gate") Teagarden.

gig: as a noun, a job, usually a one-nighter; as a verb, to play such a job.

gone: see *crazy.*

goof: to wander in attention, to fail to discharge a responsibility (also, now outmoded, to *goof off*).

groovy: a superlative applied to a music that swings, or that is *funky.*

gutbucket: early term for early earthy music (see page 101).

hame: job outside the music business.

have a ball: to enjoy oneself enormously.

head arrangement: a score put together on the spot, by the members of a band.

hip: initiated, knowing (see page 103).

horn: any instrument, not simply the brass and reeds.

hot: (now little used) once used to describe the real jazz, improvised jazz; also once used to distinguish the real jazz from the fake, and the music that swings from that which doesn't, as in *hot jazz.*

hype: as a verb, to deceive; as a noun, a form of deception.

icky: (obsolete) a *cornball*, one who does not *dig*.

Jack: the jazz equivalent of "Mac" or "Bud" in American slang; a form of address sometimes replaced by "Jim."

jam: to improvise.

jam session: a group of improvisers at work.

jazz: see Chapter 12.

jazzy: today synonymous with *corny*.

jitterbug: (obsolescent after the early forties) a frenzied jazz dancer, generally an adolescent.

jive: as a noun, comic speech, usually larded with ambiguous jazz terms; as a verb, to kid or to fool someone; as an adjective, fake.

jukebox: electrical coin machine which plays records.

jump: swing.

kicks: collective noun meaning pleasure.

kill: to fracture, to delight.

latch on: to *dig*, to *catch on;* also to become one of the party, to jump on the bandwagon.

lead: the leading or top line in any section of a band, or the man who plays that part.

leap: (obsolete) *jump*.

lick: used in early days to designate a phrase or a solo (also, *hot lick*).

long hair: classical musician or partisan of traditional music.

mickey mouse: used of an orchestra that plays *corn* or to describe some other kind of poorly contrived sound only dubiously musical in shape.

moldy fig: a modernist's name for an ardent admirer of early jazz.

Nicksieland: the somewhat modern brand of Dixieland played by small groups at Nick's, the Greenwich Village night club.

off beat: weak, unaccented beat.

out of this world: outmoded superlative.

pad: apartment, home, or bed.

pop: abbreviation of "popular song."

remote: late evening band broadcast from club, ballroom, or hotel (infrequent in present-day radio, and hence infrequently used).

rhythm-and-blues (*R and B*): elementary form of jazz, usually the blues, intended for backwoods audiences or their urban equivalents.

riff: two- or four-bar phrase.

rock: swing, jump.

salty: angry, irritated.

scat: to improvise with nonsense singing syllables; later called *bop,* or *riff,* instead of *scat,* singing.

see: to read music.

scene: a particular place or atmosphere, as for example, the "New York scene" or the "Ellington scene."

send: to stimulate, move; also one who *sends,* a *sender* (little used after the swing era).

sharp: fashionable, felicitous.

sideman: a musician in a band.

society band: inoffensive commercial band of small skill, playing for what remains of the carriage trade.

solid: superlative, swing-era version; more or less synonymous with *groovy.*

square: the uninitiated, the unknowing; one who does not *dig.*

standard: a tune that has become a jazz classic.

sweet: little used today but once widely applied to music that is played straight, without improvisation, but in which the melody can always be recognized.

swing: to get a beat, to move, a verb that developed out of that noun generally applied to music of the late 1930s; as a verb and as an adjective (*swinging*), still much used.

tag: ending added to a composition.

take five: imperative phrase meaning that one is entitled (or ordered) to take a five-minute intermission.

the end: see *crazy.*

ticky: see *corny.*

Tin Pan Alley: descriptive term for the places where popular music is composed and vended; geographically, the Broadway area in the upper 40s and lower 50s in New York.

too much: said of something so very good that it is hard to endure

it for very long without pain; in general use, just another superla‑
tive.

torch: occasionally used after the 1920s and 1930s as a description of
a ballad of unrequited love.

two beat: four-four time in which two of the beats are heavily ac‑
cented; Dixieland, New Orleans jazz.

wail: to play extremely well.

walking rhythm: a moving, four-beat rhythmic pattern, usually said
of the bass line.

wig: to *flip;* also to think with skill and precision, and (as a noun)
brain.

wild: astonishing.

world: see *scene.*

zoot: (obsolete) exaggerated clothing.

9 the morality of jazz

Those who write about jazz musicians in the public press have often been concerned about their morality. With an intensity of interest that one sometimes wishes were directed at a larger part of our culture, they have inquired searchingly into the lives, private and public, of jazzmen. Whenever anybody in jazz has been found guilty of violating the law, statutory or moral, a large fuss has accompanied the finding. It is the purpose of this chapter to develop in some detail the picture of the life of jazz musicians as it is really lived; to replace fantasies with facts, and to indicate some of the reasons for the facts.

On the whole, the moral life of a jazz musician is directed toward the same end as everybody else's: his aim is usually expressed, when he bothers to put it in words at all, as "happiness," his own and others'. He is hard put to it to define this goal in precise terms, for he has not often had to deal with the working vocabulary of moral philosophers. He is not at all sure what the nature of happiness is, although he does know that for him it is tied up with more than passing competence on his instrument, a certain amount of public recognition, and the articulate expression of his ideas on paper or on his horn, toward which most of his working, thinking, and dreaming life is directed.

The great limitation of a life with so little training, not only in moral philosophy but in any of the traditional disciplines that we call the liberal arts, is that disorganization, even chaos, may all too easily become the texture of one's life. And so it is very often with jazz musicians, who are certainly among the more disorganized members of this society—that is, in everything that is not immediately connected with their music. Such order as exists comes only, for most of them, in playing or rehearsing, in composing or arranging, or in planning to do any of these things.

The result of three or four celebrated cases of drug addiction, and of a few others that were never more than suspected, is the notion that everybody in jazz is a lowbred character, a slattern if a woman, a slavering drug addict if a man. And these fancies, unfortunately, have become a very real part of the folklore of jazz, that is, the folklore of those who know little about it but have vigorous imaginations.

Certainly many in jazz have broken rules, dishonored themselves and others, created about themselves an atmosphere at best disorderly and at worst debauched. But to generalize from these cases that every time one sees or hears a jazzman one is in the presence of evil incarnate is to belie the facts and to do violence to that basic charity without which human beings cannot live together—even in night clubs.

There are no precise estimates of good and evil in the jazz profession, any more than there are in any other. Nobody has ever attempted a large-scale sampling of the moral lives of musicians and singers, managers and bookers and band boys; the only recorded effort—made by some sociologists— was, there is every reason to believe, sabotaged by jazzmen who allowed their imagination full play in answering the questions directed to them. But all who have ever worked close to the center of the jazz world know that there is a certain amount of rottenness at that core. Beyond any question drugs have made their way into jazz, and every other sort of moral weakness has manifested itself, at one time or another, somewhere in this music. The questions to be answered, then, are these: How basic to jazz is this behavior pattern? What explains it?

Because jazz was first played in an unsavory atmosphere, for a very long time it was difficult to dissociate the music from the people for whom it was so often performed. Because the early performers were themselves untutored, the victims of a society which behind pious surface protestations led a licentious existence, there was inevitably disorganization, disorder, debauchery, in jazz in its early years. But as it became more and more clear that this was a music with its own kind of discipline, with rigorous playing and thinking demands, with something approaching an esthetic of its own— it became equally clear that it would be impossible to lead the life of dissolution and dissipation that characterized the New Orleans beginnings. And at the same time, because of the change in the nature of the music played by the second and third waves of jazzmen, a more serious, better-organized, better-educated, perhaps more sensitive sort of person began to make his way into jazz—often, it is true, to be corrupted, but at least as often to counteract the corruption of others. With new generations came new standards and an effective disjunction between those who had led the one kind of life —empty and self-centered morally, no matter how distinguished musically—and those who insisted upon the other kind—disciplined in almost every way, morally as well as musically.

This division is one that everybody in jazz knows about, although it is not often discussed. It has often made for great difficulties for members of both groups. For jazz has its own laws of survival, the result of a kind of caste system which accepts or rejects those who do or do not observe one or another standard of behavior. At the worst, these castes enforce a systematic selection of musicians which brings together those who are "on" something or other and tosses aside those who are not; "the habit" (that is, drug addiction) may very well determine a jazzman's employability, so that a very precise kind of immorality added to a certain small instrumental or singing skill may become a shortcut to success. On the other hand, it is also true that many bands are made up entirely of "clean" musicians who will not have in their ranks anybody "on" anything; these perhaps err sometimes in the other direction by refusing even to deal with a musician who has "kicked the habit," really moved outside the obsessive horrors of drug addiction.

The central explanation of the failure of jazz musicians to show much esteem for the moral life is the failure of the rest of us to give them the education they need and want. That morally impoverished attitude of the Victorians which relegated show people to a position in society only a notch higher than that of low menials has had a telling effect upon the lives of jazz musicians. It has regulated their roles in society, keeping alive poorly founded prejudices against them in schools at every level. It has made it almost impossible for them to bring together all at once that sense of moral purpose and musical order, indissolubly joined together, which, in the more traditional kinds of music, has so often been responsible for works of grandeur.

Only someone who has lived for many years close to jazz musicians can know the frustration of some of these talented people as they have tried to express ideas, feelings, insights variously vague or incisive, for which their playing and thinking and composing equipment was simply too rudimentary. Only those of us who have watched these courageous attempts of jazzmen can recognize, I think, the despondency, the sense of inadequacy, the torture, from which jazz musicians have so often suffered, which have so often sent them far beyond drink in an effort to appease their sagging spirits.

None of this should be construed as apology for misbehavior. Rather is it an explanation, without which it is impossible to understand the moral dilemmas that so often confront jazz musicians, and even the content of so much of their music. There is often a burden of frustration amounting to frenzy in the music of jazz. The weight of that burden is no more difficult for the wise and sympathetic listener to hear in jazz than it is in so-called classical music; the content in jazz is at least as meaningful an indication of the condition of a human soul as it is in the poetry of Charles Baudelaire. However small-scale the self-doubt or the frustration, the failure is a human one, and if it is effectively translated into jazz, it obviously makes for good art.

There have been attempts to organize some education for jazz musicians at various conservatories and one or two colleges. But we must go far beyond this sort of dabbling if we are to take full advantage of the great gifts with which so many in jazz have been so liberally endowed. There must be an effort to impress upon jazz musicians the fullness of that heritage in all the arts which is theirs as much as it is the poet's or painter's or symphonic composer's. We must recognize in our instruction in music in the schools just how sizable a body of expression jazz is, what its technical ramifications are, how far it reaches in ambition if not in grasp. We must encourage those who play it to analyze it and we must give them the vocabulary and training of analysis, the depth of insight which comes only with protracted examination and recognizes that in jazz, as in all art, there is symbol and metaphor, and that this apparatus of art has always been a part of jazz, however little appreciated or understood.

Such an approach to this music will result in a constantly increasing control of resources, for which so many jazz musicians since the transition years of World War II have earnestly prayed. Nor will that move toward control necessarily lessen the vitality which distinguishes jazz. Finally, in the fifties some real respect has developed for what has been called "progressive" or "modern" jazz. Some years after the best of bop and the more striking accomplishments of that revolution in thermodynamics which is called cool jazz, has come public recognition for both. Perhaps now it will be possible for jazzmen to work hard at developing further, not only improvising but knowing why and what they are improvising. Perhaps now there is some chance that they will be recognized not as pretenders to an intellectuality which is not properly theirs, but as musicians, as artists, who have every right to the ambitions of the creative spirit. As speculative musicians they have been responsible for adventurous and not altogether unsuccessful experiments, which have dotted jazz performances in concert halls and record studios and night clubs in the last fifteen years.

In order to defeat the license which must be deplored whenever and wherever it appears, in jazz or anywhere else, there must be an increase in a different kind of freedom for jazz musicians. They must be free to see themselves—and to hear themselves—as respectable members of society, decently educated, broadly equipped, disciplined in their art and in others as well. The spontaneous elements in jazz must be protected, of course, but to do so one need not obliterate the extemporizing performer's growth in wisdom and grace.

It is altogether unnecessary, then, to surround jazz and jazz musicians with an atmosphere which is a kind of musical-comedy version of a red-light district, in which everybody has the jolliest of good times playing at being gangsters and gun molls, pimps and madams and whores. The foolish romance which has so often attached itself to this reading of jazz history must be identified for what it is: a serious distortion of reality. With some recognition of what jazz has triumphed over and what it can triumphantly become, we can confidently say that a different sort of behavior pattern can be established among almost all jazz musicians.

The morality of jazz rests securely or insecurely, as the case may be, upon the receptivity of Americans to the men and women of jazz. To the extent that jazz musicians are received with responsibility and generosity by the rest of the nation they have done so much to ornament; to the extent that they are offered the same educational opportunities as fashion models and football players, airplane mechanics and telephone repairmen, poets and philosophers; to the extent that the most elementary human rights of jazz musicians are protected and their hopes and skills are regarded with something like broad human sympathies—to that extent, optimistic predictions about the morality of jazz musicians in the future can be made.

10 the profession of jazz

What sort of profession is jazz? What kind of opportunities does it hold out to aspiring musicians and to others, perhaps untalented as performers, who are anxious to get into anything connected with this music? How difficult is it to get into—or how easy? What sort of future does it offer? What security?

Jazz is today a mixture of professions, so very much a part of the entertainment world that it is difficult to say where the general lines of the amusement industry leave off and the special ones of jazz begin. It does pose its own problems, however, and suggest solutions to them; it does require particular preparation, singular skills, and something approaching dedication. For those to whom this music represents an interest amounting to addiction; for those to whom life would be really incomplete without some direct participation in jazz; for those to whom talent has been given to match this taste, the following pages offer what seem to me to be the necessary specifications for professional work in the field.

INSTRUMENTALISTS

The first and most formidable body of workers in jazz consists of musicians so equipped as to justify the really honorable title of "jazzman." The future, it seems to me, belongs to jazzmen of very large background in music, at the conservatory level or its equivalent, with a rigorous preparation in the disciplines of jazz as distinguished from any other in the art of music. More and more, jazz musicians are called upon to perform on their instruments with virtuoso ease. More and more, they are expected—almost all of them —to be soloists capable of developing original ideas on the spot. More and more, they are expected to develop at will the felicities earlier associated only with talents approaching genius.

Obviously, not every jazz musician can be expected to be thoroughly original in his thinking and to be equipped with the technique of a prodigy. But for the present, at least, those who find ready employment in jazz—as distinguished from other kinds of popular music—will be those who have the necessary rhythmic and melodic gifts, who can get over their horns with precision and polish, and who can work into all sorts of situations involving two, three, or twenty musicians without losing their freshness and spontaneity, that ready flow of ideas which marks the improvising musician. The remarkable fact—and fact it is—is that there has been an always-increasing supply of such musicians in the last two decades, and today they seem to be more numerous than ever.

Youngsters determined to make their living as jazz musicians must remember the size and scope of the education required: real distinction in jazz comes only as the result of the most enthusiastic address to the problems of jazz in particular and the puzzlements of music in general. In jazz, because it is so much a matter of extemporaneous expression, the art is continually being reconstructed, recreated, reorganized. It is worked out, then changed, rethought and redeveloped. Regularly its problems are thrashed out in bull session, in critical exchange, in letters private and public, between those who write about it and those who play it; regularly reputations are cut down as new ones are built up. The mortality rate for talent in jazz—real talent, not simply the product of press agents' dreams—is very high.

Those who go into jazz looking to make a mark today must look forward to positions not unlike those of the virtuoso pianists and violinists, great conductors, and primadonna singers of the world of classical music. They are likely to be subject to the same sort of adulation and confusion, and must be able to handle themselves before large crowds and small. They must expect to lose completely the protection of anonymity, and must be up to the rigors of a high-tension existence. In this world, there are not seven or eight or even several dozen famous names, but at the very least several hundred; and of all these many men and women the most exacting standards of performance are required by their audiences, by their fellow musicians, by the very nature of the music itself.

No amount of special pleading can indicate how vital to a jazz musician a solid education really is. For an instrumentalist who would fully develop his talents in jazz, in order to make his own contribution significant and to help make others' important too, any sort of liberal-arts preparation which leads to a firm grasp of the nature of art will be valuable. If he can combine the necessary philosophy, psychology, and technical instruction in music, he can look forward to more than just the meteoric career—quickly up and just as quickly down—which has been the fate of most jazzmen. He can expect something more than early exhaustion of his creative resources as a jazz musician, the crippling of drive and purpose and imagination which has befallen so many of the most liberally endowed jazzmen early in their careers. What I am suggesting, then, is a college education leading to graduate work in music, with as much sideline work, as many gigs, as the student can find to develop his jazz skills. Nothing so academic as a Ph.D. would make sense for a jazz musician, but there is much to be said for the kind of M.A. work that musicians such as Lennie Tristano, Dave Brubeck, and John LaPorta have done, which in no way has curbed their fecundity as improvisers.

None of this is to say that the jazz of the future will be cut and dried and academically prescribed. It will always have room for home-bred talent. There will always be room for mutations, or at least swinging mutations, for the intuitive genius, possibly self-instructed, who can fit in easily with those more formally trained. But there seems little question that as jazz develops its present-day propensity for the abstract and the atonal, the complex and the contrapuntal—as it must—it will demand the carefully tutored musician, if it is to remain fluent and fresh and moving.

One other factor must be noted—that of the disappearance, for the most part, of the fixed personnel in jazz. Less and less does a jazz musician find long-term employment with a band; more and more is he a soloist who finds occasional employment with the fluctuating personnels of the name leaders, or even one-night jobs for various booking agencies. The only permanent work that remains today in jazz is for the leader of a band of any size who himself has a substantial reputation, or for the well-known members of a small combination which by its very nature must retain its particular personnel to stay in business. Apart from this, a steady income can come only from a well-plotted piece-work existence or regular employment in the radio, television, or motion-picture studios, with occasional excursions into jazz as a means of keeping one's lips firm and one's fingers limber in the jazz manner.

If the combination of demanding requirements for significant achievement as a jazz musician, and all that is risky besides in the very nature of the profession, do not discourage one, then one may very well have the makings of a jazzman. If, in addition, one's talent is confirmed by playing experience and the encouragement of jazz musicians who can judge talent, then one certainly ought to regard oneself as a bona-fide jazz musician.

A bandleader in jazz must fulfill all the requirements for
instrumental distinction specified above and have access to
a small fortune besides. He must, in addition, be a personality
of some magnetism—that is, a musician who registers clearly
and easily with those who see and hear him, who attracts
crowds of admirers in night-club or ballroom appearances,
on the TV or motion-picture screen, and on phonograph
records.

A great investment is involved in starting—or even at-
tempting to start—a large band. Few businesses, except
those in heavy industry, need much more money to get
going than a jazz band. It is difficult enough for a dance
orchestra, with strictly box-office concerns and every sort of
good commercial prospect, to make its way from obscurity
to prominence, from the red to the black. For a jazz band,
there are additional obstacles that come from lack of interest on the part of bookers and club owners, ballroom operators and recording executives. Large new jazz bands must
somehow develop a following, demonstrate a uniqueness—
what amounts to an incontrovertible need for their existence. And new jazz bands must look forward to years of
paying off debts; if success comes, it must be sufficient to
offset losses that may run to six figures.

Only the small combination can ever get going with
small funds. Of course, this is all to the good as far as jazz
and jazzmen are concerned, for a small combination is more
manageable musically as well as financially. It can make a
living as a small-town or regional outfit without ever achiev-
ing national prominence, and can make a contribution to

music while assuring something like economic security to its participating musicians.

Still, there are many difficulties in the way of success, musical or financial, for what is called a "combo" in jazz, or for the musician, such as a pianist, who intends to work as a "single." The combo and the single must face many problems that are junior versions of those confronting a large band. But the single, like the combo, has in his favor the barroom owners and diminutive clubs who allow a certain amount of serious jazz between the acts or behind the drinkers. And if the musicians involved are up to it, with not too much effort—or rather with less than Herculean striving—something like a concert career can be molded, especially if it is combined with satisfactory club appearances.

SINGERS

It is most discouraging that nothing like an organized procedure for developing singing talent in jazz exists today. More than instrumentalists, jazz singers are expected to spring and to sing full-blown, full-grown, from obscurity. The standards by which jazz singers are judged are flexible, but tenuous too. For some, it is a matter of the beat, for others a peculiar sound that assures immediate identification. For all, it is a not easily defined magic that catches musicians' fancies and then the public's as well. Those who have achieved distinction as jazz singers range from guttural blues singers to ballad chanters capable in their mellifluous performances of at least suggesting a beat, insinuating an improvisation. Jazz has given its kudos to Jimmy Rushing, Joe Williams, Bessie Smith, and Frank Sinatra; to Mildred Bailey, Ella Fitzgerald, and Anita O'Day; to Leo Watson and Billie Holiday; to Red McKenzie and Kay Davis. There has been room all at once in jazz for a coloratura soprano—the last named—and for singers who could barely carry a tune but who have shown an unmistakable drive and wit and musical ingenuity in their handling of the melodic line.

To suggest a particular preparation for, first, the development of talent and, second, the successful sale of it, would indicate some fixed machinery by which a jazz singer of quality, musical and commercial, can be singled out. Because there really is no such apparatus, I can do no more than underline my own conviction that a jazz singer should be gifted rhythmically and melodically, should be less a legitimate, classically trained singer than a husky-voiced specialist who is fully up to improvisation with any combination of horns and regards his or her voice as the most supple of musical instruments. I can only add my devout hope that the singer will respect ordinary standards of intonation.

Getting into jazz singing professionally is chiefly a matter of developing a stoical disregard for decent food, decent lodging, and a decent income. Even less than for jazz musicians are there opportunities for jazz singers, no matter how talented. With enough skill, and a really dogged dedication to this curious part of the art of jazz, a singer may look forward to some sort of position alongside the saxophonists, the trumpeters, and the rhythm sections. But history shows that only the most determined and usually the most generously equipped have been able to come from two-bit gigs and odd week ends on the "borscht circuit" to broad prominence and high performance in jazz singing.

ARRANGERS AND COMPOSERS

In some ways these men are expected to be the most thoroughly gifted, best prepared, and most completely devoted of jazzmen. They must often turn out their scores under harrowing conditions, with not enough time to do even a hack job, and still maintain something like originality and verve in their writing. If they make their way into the greener fields of popular music, they can expect rich rewards; if they stay in jazz, they cannot expect much more than a reputation and a certain scattering of record royalties. All this, as in the case of their classical opposite numbers, the Beethovens and Mozarts, the Stravinskys and Schönbergs, in return for nothing less than genius and the willingness, nay the eagerness, to share their musical wealth freely.

If one is an arranger or composer more or less exclusively, with no particular inclination to make a living as an instrumentalist or leader, then one should go into jazz only if the musical rewards are worth all the other risks—and they are many, financial and physical, and musical as well. If one becomes efficient in the writing of jazz originals or the organization of other men's leading ideas, one must still expect to have to fight for every score that deviates in the least from the familiar and the expected; because jazz is so much a matter of on-the-spot performance, one must face a stubborn conservatism or a downright dullness, neither of which attitudes will encourage the experimental or the daring in arranging or composing jazz scores. Nonetheless, since the pioneer work of Fletcher Henderson and Duke Ellington, the arranger and the composer, united in one man or not, have become indispensable to the functioning of any large band and of many small ones. At this point in the history of jazz, one knows, if this is one's métier, that for all the heavy academic background now required and the heartbreak now assured, jazz cannot get along without the composer-arranger. Like the jazz singer, he has had to come to this field with no easily prescribed schooling, without any certainty of any future. And like the jazz singer, an arranger or composer perseveres because he may yet turn out to be a Henderson or an Ellington, a Ralph Burns or a Jack Montrose, a Dave Brubeck or a Charlie Mingus.

TEACHERS

This is in some ways the most exciting classification in the jazz profession, because it is the newest, the most rapidly growing, the most demanding, and in many ways the most satisfying. As yet there are no easy standards by which to judge the jazz teacher; the private instructor, in the art of jazz in general or of each of the instruments or singing or arranging, must himself be a highly skilled performer. He has every chance of great success if he is the leader of one or another of the schools of jazz playing or of jazz thinking. In private instruction, particularly if he holds a high place as founder or developer of a particular jazz school, he is in the position of a Socrates or one of the later leaders of the Platonic Academy, or of a Marinetti at the head of the Futurists or a Mallarmé conducting his Tuesday afternoon salon. Disciples will come to learn, to absorb everything, to follow his every word with something like slavish adoration. A teacher in this position has obvious privileges and equally clear responsibilities, and, what is more, holds on to his position whether he likes it or not, because of the particular nature of jazz, so much like the other *avant-garde* arts of the last two centuries, a profession made up of cliques and coteries, a social and musical structure which works as much to the advantage as to the disadvantage of the art.

The particular role of a teacher instructing classes in jazz at a conservatory, a college, a university, or a high school is very different from that of the private man and even less clearly defined. This is a developing position for which no set of requirements could have been laid down. Wherever possible, institutions are making use of musicians who have had at least rudimentary jazz-playing experience. And, best of all, specialized schools of jazz are being formed with spacious, well-planned curricula. These institutions in future years may become the nuclei of graduate schools in jazz, fully capable of educating an instrumentalist, a leader, an arranger, composer, or singer, and of providing the music with succeeding generations of teachers really trained in the art of tutoring others, not merely of graduating from performer to professor.

MANAGERS, BOOKERS, ETC.

Those responsible for the business end of jazz must be businessmen. If they are not professed as personal managers or road managers, as bookers or press agents, ballroom or night-club operators, theater or concert-hall managers, or band boys. they will not have much to offer the leaders whom they serve or hire or enslave. There is room at this end of the profession of jazz for creative talent too, for those with sympathy for the music, or, better still, background in it. Some unusual men and women stand out in this field, if not for their every effort at least for the bulk of their work in support of the work of others. The devotion to a particular musician on the part of a particular manager or booker or press agent is very touching to experience. Such people often develop an understanding of jazz that matches or exceeds that of many jazzmen; they couple musical with economic judgment. One can only hope that as a youngster makes his way into this necessary part of jazz, even as a band boy, doing the countless manual labors of that general factotum, he will educate himself in what might be called a vital craft, since it really can help assure the integrity of the art it supports. No particular preparation can be pointed to except the general self-tutoring suggested here, but that is a kind of education after all.

RECORD-COMPANY EXECUTIVES, A AND R MEN

Of all the business associations with jazz, at once the most gratifying and the most frustrating is that of the record-company executive or the A and R man, the recording supervisor whose initials stand for "artists and repertory." These important figures in the industry have much to do with the choice of tunes, selection of bands and singers and solo musicians, and creation of policy and pattern in their companies' recording programs. On them depends much of the success or failure of jazz at any given time. While they cannot altogether command public taste, they can do more to form it than anyone else in music, including the musician.

By the very nature of their profession, the executive behind the desk and the supervisor in the control room must be primarily concerned with sales figures. They may be acutely disturbed by one performer and deeply moved by another, but they cannot reject the one and support the other on the basis of their own tastes or what they may know to be solid musical standards—not on these alone, in any case. The ultimate measurements are the spinnings of the records in the jukeboxes and on the disk jockeys' turntables, the numbers that are sold across the record counters. With these large factors in mind, A and R men and their business associates can retain their jobs in the billion-dollar music industry and some share of the billion.

No particular background will guarantee employment in one of these lucrative positions or assure success in it. The record-company executive is usually a businessman who has some connection, vague or quite specific, with music. He may once have been a bandleader or a booker of bands. He may, on the other hand, have sold men's or women's clothing, have been attached to a Hollywood film company or a New York bank. The A and R man almost always has had a more direct association with music, often with jazz of quality, as performer, arranger, critic, writer for a trade publication, or owner of a record shop which produced records of some jazz importance.

These specifications are meant to apply to those who work in and for the large companies. Those who start their own small record labels can make their own rules. For with the small companies, personal tastes and musical standards can be respected and served; with these organizations the only frustrations to which one need look forward are the financial.

CRITICS, REVIEWERS, EDITORS

These figures, almost as well known to the jazz public as those they write about, have been dealt with in the chapter on the schools of jazz. Here it must be pointed out that while there are not many jobs of this kind in jazz, those that are available do require more and more particular preparation, and do offer, at the same time, particular pleasures. A jazz critic, like a jazz teacher, exerts an enormous influence. He cannot often make or break a record or a club engagement, as the New York drama critics can often establish or close a play; but he can do much to open or close the ears of his readers to new kinds of music. He plays, over and over again, a formidable role in that constant exchange of opinion and fancy, of well-backed judgment and empty allegation, which makes the pages of the leading and the lesser jazz journals, here and abroad, so engaging to read. For this is a music as alive in the discussion as in the performance, in which words bring blood to the head almost as easily as the music sends a beat to the feet.

One can only hope that those who make themselves or are made critics, and those who perform the less free-wheeling functions of the reviewer or the more responsible overseership of the editor, will in future prepare themselves as thoroughly as possible for their work. This preparation is not simply a matter of journalism school or music courses. It involves the steady frequenting of the places where jazz is played and a very close acquaintance with jazz musicians.

It demands the same sort of general background that the first-rate instrumentalist in the jazz to come will have to possess: a broad education in the liberal arts. It asks, on every level, for an open-mindedness which can serve a music that is constantly growing and has not yet made altogether clear its limitations or its longevity.

Comparatively free from the pressures of advertisers and publishers, the man who finds himself a member of the working press of jazz will discover a critical liberty such as no other art can offer. He may not be up to lifetime employment in the field: it takes the utmost physical and intellectual and spiritual strength to last out even a few years of record or club reviewing and of writing more general critical articles. But however long he spends in the field, if his preparation is up to a performance of quality, he will find that he has been working close to the center of all art; he will know that his experience has been a vital one in the development of the creative intelligence, his own and others', and he will be content to have made that contribution, however small the financial reward. For jazz offers him what it offers everybody at some point in the profession: the sense of being alive in a singularly lively art which has remained that way and, as long as it stays itself, will continue that way, for its particular identifying characteristic, after all, is spontaneity.

11 the judging of jazz

For Plato the judging of music was simple: some harmonies were effeminate and convivial, some plaintive, some violent, some tranquil. One was a success or a failure as a composer or performer to the extent that one chose correctly from a small number of modes for a small number of purposes. For us it is a great deal more difficult: there is no such simple identification of sound and purpose for our composing or performing or listening.

If our listening is instructed by any set of conventions, it is equally taught by temperament and taste. We rarely react to music the same way twice, even when we have a composer's declared intention before us and a technical knowledge of what he has accomplished in his music. Now if that is true of performances limited by fixed notes on paper and firm traditions in the execution of those notes, how much more will it be true of jazz, in which each performance is designed to be different from every other!

How, then, in a sea of shifting values, in which change seems to be all that is constant, do we ever make judgments? Our most important answer comes, I think, when we recognize that not everything does change in jazz. There are certain elements in jazz sufficiently alike to be called constant, from performance to performance, from school to school, from instrument to instrument. The identification of these elements makes an excellent starting place for any valid value judgment in jazz.

Certain of these elements are central to all music. We should be concerned, for example, with identifying the technical background of a performer, in jazz as elsewhere; we must know, through our own ears or those of others, something of a performer's grasp of harmonic and melodic and rhythmic essentials. Even with the peculiar approach of jazzmen to pitch and color, we should be able to describe with some accuracy the intonation and attack of this or that performer on this or that instrument, or of whole sections or whole bands. It is possible to detect the steadiness or unsteadiness of beat of a jazzman, whether in a rhythm section or not. And finally, even within the enormous restrictions of words, some of the characteristic resonances and timbres of individual players can be sketched in outline, or drawn with some degree of identifying detail.

We have in jazz today, too, something that might be called a first cousin to tradition: the variety of styles that have developed around the playing and singing of the blues, around certain New Orleans classics for those who play in the Dixieland tradition, or around songs such as "I Got Rhythm," "Back Home in Indiana," "How High the Moon," "Lullaby of Birdland," "Moonlight in Vermont," "Foggy Day," "Don't Blame Me," "Embraceable You," and "All the Things You Are"—tunes that we associate with dozens of different approaches to jazz, from swing to the most advanced jazz counterpoint. In the bop era, with certain sets of figures, such as "Hothouse" and "Donna Lee," "Groovin' High," and "Ko-Ko," went certain ways of playing, built around the solos of Charlie Parker and Dizzy Gillespie. In later years other tunes have become permanently attached to other personalities. None perhaps is as irresistibly associated with a performer in the jazz listener's mind as "Body and Soul" with Coleman Hawkins in the swing era or almost any part of his whole repertory with Charlie Parker today, but all are unmistakably tied to one jazzman or another. All background material can be scrutinized in describing new performances of old tunes; at least as much of it as is clearly relevant can be examined. This may be a nuisance in the normal execution of reviewing duties or in the quick consideration of an addition to one's record library; but in the more extended evaluation of a significant performer or performance, such comparative history is extremely valuable.

Once one has approached the forms of jazz with this many facts in mind, it is possible to indulge fancy. Then one can begin to attack the elusive problems of content in jazz. One can examine the kinds of emotion, no matter how thoroughly personal, that may be elicited by a given piece of music. With all the necessary limitations in mind, one can classify the degrees of excitement or the grades of assuagement; the brightness or fullness of a particular kind of chord; the moods evoked by long melodic lines thoroughly consonant in texture or by more dissonant short ones. One may discover that a certain solidity in scoring or a particular looseness will correspond to some sequence of emotions. One may find that incisive statements of melody are bracing or that diffuse ones cause the attention to wander and utterly disengage the emotions.

This is an intensely subjective set of responses to jazz that I have been describing, but it is a very important one. It involves highly individual thresholds of pleasure and pain, very personal definitions of musical right and wrong, and assertions of taste and distaste of which there may be as many as there are listeners to jazz. To make sense out of one's emotions as they are aroused by jazz, one must be willing to develop a kind of introspection in which those emotions are constantly subject to rigorous analysis, analysis more intellectual than most people like to give their emotions. The end product of such self-examination is usually recognition that the borderline between emotions and intellect barely exists, at least as far as the knowing response to an art is concerned, even to an art that, like jazz, seems so much of the time to be largely directed at the emotions.

Sooner or later one does recognize, in any serious attempt to organize one's reactions to jazz, that this is a highly intellectual procedure which requires unfailing self-discipline not unlike that to which the jazz musician regularly subjects himself. The inspiration for such discipline must ultimately be the quality of the music itself and the conviction that there really are high technical standards in jazz, supported by sensitive performers who have a clear goal to which their performances can and should be directed.

What is the goal of the jazz musician? If it can be named, obviously much of what we have been talking about can be examined in the light of a jazzman's success or failure in reaching that goal and in terms of a jazz listener's ability to follow him along the way. It is audacious to attempt to define any simple, uniform goal as the end purpose of all jazz musicians. Nevertheless it is an attempt I must make, for it seems clear to me that whatever other intentions may outwardly occupy the jazzman's playing and inwardly command his thinking and feeling about his music, one central concern animates him beyond all others. This can be summed up in a word that is familiar enough: development. Jazz, in common with a great many other arts in our time, has ceaselessly exercised itself over the need to go forward. To make progress is the great aim of most jazz musicians today. No dimension of time holds such allure for them as the future; no condemnation seems so terrible to them as that of being "dated."

At its worst this preoccupation with forward movement settles into a debilitating courtship of the merely novel in jazz. At its best it accounts for a profound probing of materials which can make a close encounter with the jazzman's mind a remarkably stimulating experience. No matter how ruthlessly the well-equipped self-analyst in jazz disposes of the recent past as archaic or outmoded; no matter how warped his historical sense, he does have firm hold on the central fact about jazz: it is an improvised music. It is here that judgment becomes arduous, if not altogether frustrating. Here we must ask questions about the construction of a jazz performance that are almost unanswerable, sending us back again and again to the performance itself. No matter how willing the performer may be to talk about what he has done, he will not easily find the words to describe his achievement if it really is an achievement; the music will have to speak for itself.

It is best, then, at this point to recognize the limitations of the jazz musician, the jazz critic, the jazz audience. We can make statements about certain fixed technical elements in jazz. We can establish some comparative history in the performance of a tune or construction of a style or development of a playing personality. We can make some effort to sort out our own emotional responses to the music. Then we must come to this element of the jazz musician's self-examination, his self-development, his relentless concern with the materials of jazz and his conquest of them.

Jazz may not always be so deeply engrossed in the examination of itself. But as it stands now, any judgment of this music must ultimately face this fact—and not only face it but be pleased with it. Anyone who wants to spend much time with jazz must recognize that almost all of a jazz musician's energies and talents are directed toward the systematic exploration of his music and hence of himself. No figure so well sums up the position of the modern jazzman as the seated Buddha thoughtfully observing his navel. If this sort of preoccupation, thoroughly self-centered in the fascination the performer finds in his own personality and at the same time selfless in the jazzman's analytical concern for the whole art of music—if this sort of concentration in any way offends one, then one ought to begin one's judgment of jazz by judging oneself uninterested.

12 the place of jazz

The distinction between major and minor art naturally concerns anyone who writes about jazz or any other kind of music. At the same time one must be suspicious of rating systems in any discussion of the arts. Any numerical means of distinguishing one work of art from another is necessarily questionable, for it presupposes a mathematical content that can be set forth with some precision by an accountant-critic who can tote up, mechanically add or subtract, the virtues and vices, achievements and failures, of a work of art. It is important, however, to note certain general characteristics about jazz, not at all mechanical in nature, which may go some of the way toward indicating its major or minor status.

If the art of jazz is only as important as the arts of faïence or petit point, of etched glass or bagpipe music, then we should know it and make our judgments accordingly. If, on the other hand, it has at least some of the significance of that chamber music which composers in the tradition of Haydn and Mozart or Beethoven and Brahms have written for string instruments, or if it is of the order of lyric poetry or landscape or portrait painting, then this we certainly should know and accordingly find our values in jazz at a correspondingly elevated level.

It is not easy to track down those defining characteristics by which we can assign to jazz the importance of a major art or the comparative unimportance of a minor. But certain things are clear. First of all, obviously, jazz is a form of music; any consideration must put it under that general classification. And second, since it is a kind of music, then it is a kind of art. Only the most unreconstructed Philistines, I think, will deny the assertions of the self-evident here.

But what kind of music is jazz? How different is it from other kinds of music? Is there anything about it that at any time moves it, whether boldly or timidly, from the province of music across and into the precincts of any other art? My answer to all of these questions would be that jazz is, in almost all its details, of a piece with the rest of music, that it organizes sounds according to the procedures of Western music. It has been, for the most part, a thoroughly conventional kind of diatonic music, made up of combinations of half tones and whole tones, with the same tendencies to the polytonal and the atonal which all our music has had in our time, although certainly jazz has arrived at these notions a great deal later than its more experimental older brothers,

and its musicians still, perhaps, feel a little uneasy with
them. To the extent that any music sometimes sets words or
narrates a story, jazz is some of the time literary, some of
the time pictorial, some of the time concerned with translations of elements in space into sound, sometimes with
translations of events in time into what reads like a contradic-
tion in terms, but isn't: aural pictographs. It is concerned
with the same problems of conveying meaning and truth
with which all of music is beset: one never knows for sure
the precise intention of a serious jazz composer or performer; one never knows with certainty whether it is a
purely subjective speculation of the jazzman or a description of an object which should be recognizable to the hearer.
The definite and the indefinite both struggle for the jazz
musician's attention just as they do for the classical man's;
the jazz musician's listeners are left just as the classical
musician's are, sometimes satisfied, sometimes bewildered,
by what jazz evokes for them of person or place, mood or
atmosphere or precise meaning.

There are, of course, among those who listen to jazz, all
kinds of people, variously emotional or cerebral, some most
fluently associative in their listening, some more directly
musical. Jazz elicits from listeners its share of visual images,
just as other forms of music do. Jazz makes its appeal to
stock emotional responses, invoking sorrow or joy, the
maudlin or the madcap, the terrified or the delighted, just as
other music does some of the time. And jazz also can draw
to itself musically intuitive listeners, who respond to its
sounds with some apparatus which those who have it will
recognize as the musical faculty. To them, technical dis-

tinctions of form are uppermost, and yet there is some un-mistakable content as well, however difficult it may be to make verbal distinctions between the two.

Perhaps the most significant point about jazz as an art form is this: at its best what it communicates cannot be communicated in any other way; to those who know it well there is such a thing as the jazz experience, one which is entirely different from any other in music. It is this experience which draws the most intense support from jazz musicians and jazz fans.

By definition the jazz experience cannot be translated altogether successfully into words. If it could, there would be no need for jazz. All one can do, really, is select general descriptive headings that permit one to point to now one set of responses, now another, and the different sorts of music which summon them forth.

Much of jazz is concerned with the simple communication of simple pleasures. Its little masters have presented miniatures of sound, terse or somewhat more rambling, which declare that this or that kind of good time has been enjoyed. Not only do they declare that a good time has been had: they make some attempt to share it. Often the sort of three- or four- or five-minute ecstasy thus communicated does not rise above the most elementary physiological level. But some of the time there is a small poetry of pleasure of which the jazz musician is capable, which he can not only feel but re-feel, can react to not only once but several times. As he sorts out his feelings and reactions, he can think his way through to felicitous reconstructions of experience which many of us are very glad to have.

Occasionally there have been attempts at large-scale expression and development of ideas in some complexity over a considerable range of melody and harmony and rhythm. The starting point for this sort of work is almost invariably a fairly extended meditation or contemplation of the life of the jazz musician or of the Negro people in the United States, or a part of a big town, or life in all the cities of the United States, even sometimes the more abstract speculation about the nature of man or God or the relationship between the two. It would be foolish to assert that any large degree of success has attended these unsystematic expatiations upon the obvious. But the systematic and the organic have not altogether eluded the jazz musician. He will not always be confined to an abbreviated discourse and therefore in the larger forms to a kind of fragmentary anthologizing. For there is a reality packed away in the music of jazz, a reality to which millions respond with recognition if not always with pleasure. Jazz stirs certain feelings which are apparently universal. As few arts have in our time, it has been accepted internationally; it has evoked in Europe and Asia, in South America and Australia and Africa, essentially the same reaction that it has in its native North America. It obviously expresses something that audiences in the twentieth century want to have expressed for them.

It is not too difficult to point to what jazz does that so delights its millions. It is a big-city music. It reflects, as few other arts in our time do, the massiveness and the matter, the chaos and the conflicts, the frantic pace and the fragmentary nature of life as it is lived by the millions gathered together in the cliff dwellings of the modern metropolis. It does more, too, than merely reflect these elements of urban existence: it sorts them out, distinguishing certain kinds of individuals from the crowd, and saying something about each of them. And with all the poignancy of any of the arts of our time which has sought to chronicle urban life, it describes the loneliness of the big-city dweller.

For this reason it is to jazz that composers have turned when they have wanted to express these typical characteristics of life in the big twentieth-century town. The pages of jazz in the work of Stravinsky and Ravel, of Bloch and Vaughan Williams and Prokofiev, point unmistakably to such a programmatic purpose. In the same way the writer of musical cues for radio or television or motion pictures turns to jazz for this sort of urban atmosphere. And so, too, some poets have turned to jazz to build the impression of a life of rhythmic impulse, more or less subtle; in T. S. Eliot's *The Waste Land,* in the more obvious poetry of Carl Sandburg, and in some of the more recondite lines of E. E. Cummings, jazz is used as a primary or secondary resource to convey an unmistakable meaning.

The effectiveness of jazz in such a context is illustrated by that wistful strain of the blues with which Tyrone Guthrie brought to an end his Old Vic revival of Shakespeare's *Troilus and Cressida* in Edwardian dress, or by the acid commentary on life in the inflation-twisted Germany just after the First World War in Kurt Weill's *Threepenny Opera.* In painting too, in the work of such men as Stuart Davis and Byron Browne, jazz has appeared most persuasively, as symbol or metaphor of direct narrative subject. This is not what some would call the "pure" use of jazz; such painting or music is at least at one remove from the improvisation of "the real jazz." Nonetheless, it is a utilization of the resources without which much of the art of our time would be considerably poorer. Even at some distance from the playing processes of jazz, it is possible to make good use of its content; but how much better the direct use of its materials by its most seasoned, its most gifted performers!

There is at least as much skillful commentary on early and late hours, on life uptown and downtown and midtown, on every aspect of life in the big city, in the music of Duke Ellington as in that of any contemporary composer in the classical tradition. There is more wisdom about life as it is lived in the metropolis to be gathered nightly from the spontaneous outbursts of small chamber groups in jazz than is to be found in, say, Maurice Ravel's *Blue Sonata* or in those late piano sonatas of Sergei Prokofiev in which the swinging strains of jazz appear. It is a confined sort of wisdom I am talking about here; I am not comparing all the insights of this composer or that with those of the jazz improviser. But what the jazz musician, speaking directly from his own experience, has to say is very special and quite enlightening. To neglect his communication is to turn away, with a recluse's distaste for his own time, from one of the central sets of facts about the twentieth century.

Jazz musicians do know more than one environment; large numbers of them come from small towns and villages, from the farm and the ranch. But it is usually in a night club, recording studio, ballroom, or hotel that a jazzman finds himself as a jazz musician. In these places jazz is played by professionals, and it is to them that an aspiring jazzman must go, not merely for recognition, but for survival in jazz. And so it is the atmosphere of these places and all that surrounds them that the jazzman soaks up and squeezes out in his playing; it is this environment that he reproduces simply

and openly or upon which he makes more extended notes
and comment. At his best he is severely conscious of the
limitations of this environment and accepts them as necessary. In doing so he performs that conscious act of the will
and develops that precise sort of control which together mark
the genuine artist in any art form. As that control increases
and the jazz musician more and more conforms his will to
the limitations of his art, his music becomes more and more
an art. For with control and acceptance of limitation comes
an apparatus of sign and symbol without which no art of
consequence has ever existed. The intimate reflections and
secret experiences of the jazz musician can then be communicated with some certainty of understanding. Something
of this translation of intimacies has already occurred in
jazz: there are large numbers of people who really do "dig"
the arcana of jazz; its *aficionados* really have found something in jazz which cannot be found precisely in the same
detail anywhere else. The "something" which is unique to
jazz may be as yet nothing more than the passing reflections
of typical New Yorkers or Chicagoans, Los Angelenos or
Kansas Citians, or those who travel between these cities and
others. Because they are miniature, these reflections do not
canvass the sublime, except in the breach; most of the time
one knows little of real exaltation in jazz. Still, what is said
is said with conviction, and it rings true; a world of vital experience has been put together, piecemeal.

The fitting together of small pieces does not make for
a major art, although it may be from time to time the secondary function of a major art. If those small pieces are all that
a particular group of artists and their audiences have experienced with any great depth of feeling; if this is all they

really know about and can talk or dream about, then this must be their expression, their art, no matter how minor. It is to the everlasting credit of jazz that it has made its piece-work so compelling to its ardent admirers that for many of them there is no more satisfactory expression in the arts, major or minor. The distinction between ecstasy and exaltation could not concern them less. They are content with an iconography of the subway and the department store, the night club and the radio and the tabloid newspaper. They are more than content, they are thrilled, that the common-places of big-city life have been translated with such clarity into a set of sounds and that the work of translation can apparently be expected to go on forever—or at least as long as the cities in which they live go on. Jazz is, then, neither faïence nor petit point, neither etching upon glass nor the music of bagpipes. It is an art that says some of the things that must be said about this society. Ours may be a minor civilization, but to the extent that one of its particular creations, jazz, expresses it with some thoroughness, this creation has a major contribution to make and possesses a universal importance, for our time at the very least.

APPENDIX A

the musicians of jazz

NOTE: *This list has been made as comprehensive as possible; unfortunately a few names have had to be omitted because the information available was insufficient.*

ADDERLEY, Julian "Cannonball." ALTO SAXOPHONE. B. Tampa, Fla., 1928. Developed in high school and Army bands. New York debut with Oscar Pettiford (1955); later success with group led by himself and brother Nat. Much influenced by Charlie Parker.

ADDERLEY, Nat. CORNET and TRUMPET. B. Tampa, Fla., 1931. Much the same background as his brother, also played with the Lionel Hampton band in 1954-55, including Hamp's tour of Europe and Israel. Bop influences.

ALBAM, Manny. BARITONE SAXOPHONE and ARRANGER. B. Dominican Republic, 1922. Bands: Bob Chester, Georgie Auld, Charlie Barnet. From 1955 on, much recorded as arranger, especially for Joe Newman on Victor.

ALEXANDER, Elmer "Mousie." DRUMS. B. Gary, Ind., 1922. After two years with Jimmy McPartland's group (1948-50), moved to wife Marian's in the mid-fifties; later Sauter-Finegan and

Benny Goodman bands. Notably tasteful small-group drummer of modern school.

ALLEN, Henry "Red" Jr. TRUMPET. B. Algiers, La., 1908. Famous son of famous father (who led the Excelsior Brass Band), Red went up north with Fate Marable's river boat band, joined King Oliver in Chicago (1927) and then Luis Russell (1929). Brilliant, driving performances with Fletcher Henderson (1933), Blue Rhythm (1934-1936), Louis Armstrong (1937-40), own bands; for years co-leader with Jay C. Higginbotham.

AMMONS, Albert. PIANO. B. Chicago, Ill., 1907. One of the first and most durable of the boogie-woogie pianists. Led a particularly effective small band at the Club DeLisa in Chicago (1934-38).

AMMONS, Eugene. TENOR SAXOPHONE. B. Chicago, Ill., 1925. Son of Albert. One of the most successful of the bop tenor men; with Billy Eckstine 1944-47; his own groups afterward, including a two-year band co-led with Sonny Stitt. Versatile, of no one school but close to Lester Young.

ANDERSON, Ivy. SINGER. B. Gilroy, Calif., 1904; d. Los Angeles, Calif., 1949. Duke Ellington's distinguished singer from 1931 to 1942. As much a part of the Ellington sound in those years as any of the famous soloists.

ANDERSON, William "Cat." TRUMPET. B. Greenville, S.C., 1916. Startling high-note performer made famous in his years with Ellington (1944-47 and after 1950 again).

ARBELLO, Fernando. TROMBONE. B. Puerto Rico, 1907. Bouncy little musician, a familiar part of the orchestras of Chick Webb 1935), Fletcher Henderson (1936-37), Lucky Millinder (1937), and in the mid-forties with Jimmie Lunceford.

ARCHEY, James. TROMBONE. B. Norfolk, Va., 1902. Very much a part of the jazz scene in the 1930s (Luis Russell, Willie Bryant, Benny Carter, etc.). Afterward Europe and then small bands of New Orleans type in New York.

ARMSTRONG, Lilian Hardin. PIANO. B. Memphis, Tenn., 1903. King

Oliver's pianist (1920), then husband Louis Armstrong's (1925); later organized many dates for Decca. In 1952 went to Europe.

ARMSTRONG, Louis. TRUMPET. B. New Orleans, La., 1900. One of the great names of jazz, Louis started with a bang at a New Year's Eve celebration when he was thirteen: he shot off a gun and was sent to the Waifs' Home, in the brass band of which he developed his considerable talents for the first time. Then came further progress under the tutelage of King Oliver, whom he joined in Chicago in 1922. He played with Fletcher Henderson in 1924, organized his own Hot Five and Hot Seven into flexible recording groups particularly well directed as backgrounds for his own improvising skills. From 1929 he played off and on with the Luis Russell orchestra (which took his name). He was an enormous success in European tours in 1932 and again from 1933 to 1935, and was very much a part of the swing years in the United States. Whatever concessions he may have made to public taste as singer, trumpeter, and leader of small bands, Louis's continued control of his horn and his much abused vocal chords is demonstrated in records made as late as the mid-fifties. The best of his recent ones is probably *Armstrong Plays W. C. Handy* on Columbia.

ARODIN, Sidney. CLARINET. New Orleans, La., 1901-48. Able small-band performer in native town and Chicago; composer, with Hoagy Carmichael, of "Lazy River."

ASHBY, Irving. GUITAR. B. Somerville, Mass., 1920. Well-educated musician particularly well known for his work with Lionel Hampton's first bands (1940-42) and with the King Cole Trio (1947-50). One of the first to demonstrate the scope of the guitar as a solo instrument in modern jazz.

AULD, Georgie. TENOR SAXOPHONE. B. Toronto, Ontario, 1919. Made his first impression with the Bunny Berigan band (1937), was a vital part of Artie Shaw's 1938-39 organization and of Benny Goodman's sextet in 1940-41. His 1944-46 big band was one of the first big ones to demonstrate the large potentialities of modern jazz. In recent years his big sound, much influenced by

Coleman Hawkins, has been heard in night clubs he has managed, and on records of various kinds.

AUSTIN, Lovie. PIANO. B. Nashville, Tenn., 1895. An accompanist for such significant early blues singers as Ida Cox, Chippie Hill, and Ma Rainey.

BABASIN, Harry. BASS. B. Dallas, Texas, 1921. A West Coast fixture particularly well known for his work with Boyd Raeburn (1945) and for many date records thereafter, including a variety on cello.

BAILEY, Mildred. SINGER. B. Tekoah, Wash., 1907; d. New York, 1951. Perhaps the first to occupy the job of jazz singer with a band, with Whiteman in 1929. Later co-leader of a fine, sensitive middle-sized band with husband Red Norvo (1936-39). Gifted with a delicate sense of phrase, she rarely missed any nuance of melody or lyric and showed unusual acumen in her choice of musicians for records, radio, clubs, or theater engagements.

BAILEY, William "Buster." CLARINET. B. Memphis, Tenn., 1902. Fletcher Henderson's striking, long-time (1923-34), technically able clarinetist; not without a certain jazz feeling. Before and after with a variety of groups, notably in recent years with Red Allen.

BAKER, Chesney "Chet." TRUMPET. B. Yale, Okla., 1929. Made his reputation on the West Coast with Gerry Mulligan in 1952. Since then a familiar soft-voiced singer and a trumpeter at possibly even lower volume, leading his own small bands and recording organizations of various sizes. The epitome of cool trumpet.

BAKER, Harold "Shorty." TRUMPET. B. St. Louis, Mo., 1914. Broad experience, including Fate Marable, Don Redman, Teddy Wilson, Andy Kirk, and various engagements with Duke Ellington from 1938 to the early fifties. Recognizably superior to most in the fullness and precision of his tone.

BALL, Ronald. PIANO. B. Birmingham, England, 1927. One of Lennie Tristano's talented students (he came to the States and Lennie's studio in 1952). Several recording and club engagements with Lee Konitz.

BANK, Danny. BARITONE SAXOPHONE. B. Brooklyn, N.Y., 1922. An able anchor man with Charlie Barnet, Benny Goodman, Jimmy Dorsey, Tommy Dorsey, etc.

BAQUET, George. CLARINET. B. New Orleans, La., 1883. A big brass-band man in the first decades of this century in his native town. Later well known in Philadelphia.

BARBARIN, Paul. DRUMS. B. New Orleans, La., 1901. Luis Russell's drummer for over ten years until 1939. More recently in New Orleans, and with Dixieland outfits in New York. A veteran whose playing experience includes at least several engagements with King Oliver in Chicago.

BARBER, Bill. TUBA. B. Hornell, N.Y., 1920. Turned bleats into beats with Claude Thornhill, Miles Davis, the Sauter-Finegan band, and Pete Rugolo in the forties and fifties.

BARKER, Danny. GUITAR. B. New Orleans, La., 1909. A veteran who managed to play successfully through most of the eras of jazz from the early thirties until the present. Most recently with Paul Barbarin's group on banjo.

BARNET, Charlie. ALTO, TENOR, SOPRANO SAXOPHONES. B. New York, N.Y., 1913. Leader of successful swing band from 1932 until the early forties. An ardent proselytizer for the music of Duke Ellington in the thirties and early forties. A vivid personality on and off his several instruments, and distinguished for his support of mixed bands. His practical support: he employed and featured musicians such as Peanuts Holland and Oscar Pettiford.

BASIE, William "Count." PIANO. B. Redbank, N.J., 1906. Basie's story is band's story. After a New York gigging background he took over Bennie Moten's band after Moten's death in 1935. For the rest of the important Basie history, see Chapter 1.

BAUDUC, Ray. DRUMS. B. New Orleans, La., 1909. Bob Crosby band's drummer (1935-42), earlier with Ben Pollack and Dorsey brothers; later a West Coast fixture. A swinging Dixielander.

BAUER, Billy. GUITAR. B. New York, N.Y., 1915. After desultory beginnings he established himself as one of the most solid of rhythm men with Woody Herman (1944-46). Afterward closely associated with Lennie Tristano and the studios.

BECHET, Sidney. soprano saxophone, clarinet. B. New Orleans, La., 1897. Controversial figure of remarkable longevity as a jazz musician of prominence. Bechet had much to do with the formulation of the grooviest of the saxophone blues styles in the twenties and thirties. Best known during those years for his association with Noble Sissle (1928-38). Most recently a music-hall and jazz favorite in France. Distinguishing marks: a shivering vibrato and a beat.

BEIDERBECKE, Leon Bismarck "Bix." cornet. B. Davenport, Iowa, 1903; d. New York, N.Y., 1931. Cornet titan of the late 1920s, Bix loomed large above his associates in the Jean Goldkette and Paul Whiteman orchestras and all those assembled for record dates with him by Frankie Trumbauer and others. His exquisite tone and drive were matched by a melodic imagination close to the impressionist composers whose music he imitated on his horn and piano. The circumstances attendant upon his death by pneumonia have added to a romantic story much colored with the atmosphere of prohibition days, gangsters, ladies of the evening, and like melodramatic detail.

BELLSON, Louis. drums. B. Rock Falls, Ill., 1924. One of the power-house men of modern jazz with a florid drumming background (Benny Goodman, Tommy Dorsey, Harry James, Duke Ellington).

BERIGAN, Roland Bernard "Bunny." trumpet. B. Falls Lake, Wis., 1909; d. New York, N.Y., 1942. A superb lower-register trumpeter with a battling personality that emerged, in music, in rich playing and singing colors. After jobs with sweet bands (Kemp, Vallee, Rich) came the Dorseys and Benny Goodman and his own free-swinging band.

BERMAN, Saul "Sonny." trumpet. B. New Haven, Conn., 1924; d. New York, N.Y., 1947. Musicians made up many nicknames to describe his delightful personality when he was with Woody

Herman (from 1945 until his death). Nobody has yet described altogether successfully his felicitous style, one of the best of the modern brass styles, neat, multifaceted, swinging.

BERNHART, Milt. TROMBONE. B. Valparaiso, Ind., 1926. Stan Kenton's mainstay from 1946 until 1951; afterward a West Coast ornament notable for his melodic invention.

BERRY, Emmett. TRUMPET. B. Macon, Ga., 1916. After an early apprenticeship with the Henderson brothers and Teddy Wilson, Emmett brought his bumptious personality to bear upon many bands, at greatest length with Count Basie (1945-50). A groovy musician who has grown with jazz.

BERRY, Leon "Chu." TENOR SAXOPHONE. B. Wheeling, W. Va., 1910; d. Conneaut, Ohio, 1941. An auto crash brought to an early death one of the most imaginative of the Hawkins-like tenor men of the thirties. Chu made his great impression successively with Fletcher Henderson and Cab Calloway (1937-41) and on many, many record sessions. One of the distinctive long-line improvisers.

BERT, Eddie. TROMBONE. B. Yonkers, N.Y., 1922. A modern barrelhouse musician who trained with Red Norvo in the early forties, then developed with Woody Herman, Stan Kenton, and a variety of gig bands, some of which he has led himself.

BEST, Denzil De Costa. DRUMS. B. New York, N.Y., 1917. Most facile and most delicate small-band drummer, particularly well known for his work with the George Shearing Quintet (1949-52).

BIGARD, Leon Albany "Barney." CLARINET. B. New Orleans, La., 1906. A Dixielander with depth, Barney made rich contributions to Duke Ellington performances from 1928 to 1942; after 1946 became a Louis Armstrong sideman of distinction. Though influenced by his early surroundings, he has always stayed close to new ideas in jazz and wherever possible has made accommodations in his limpid style for them.

BISHOP, Wallace. DRUMS. B. Chicago, Ill., 1906. An Earl Hines standby for many years in the 1930s.

BISHOP, Walter, Jr. PIANO. B. New York, N.Y., 1927. One of the better boppers, second generation.

BLAKEY, Art. DRUMS. B. Pittsburgh, Pa., 1919. Billy Eckstine's solid support in the rhythm section (1944-47). Later with Buddy De Franco and his own groups, with the last of which, the Jazz Messengers, he has displayed some of the virtuosity which makes him one of the first drum soloists of real distinction on his instrument.

BLANTON, Jimmy. BASS. B. St. Louis, Mo., 1919; d. Los Angeles, Calif., 1942. The man who brought the bass alive for modern jazz, for soloists, for all who would take advantage of the vast resources of this instrument which he revealed and helped to develop in his few years with Duke Ellington (1939 until his death of tuberculosis in 1942). An enormous tone, an extraordinary sense of time, and precise technique were among the identifying characteristics of this great jazz musician.

BOLDEN, Buddy. CORNET. New Orleans, La., 1878-1931. Legendary barber turned horn blower and band leader, Bolden died of an illness that started as a bad earache.

BOSE, Sterling Belmont. TRUMPET. B. New Orleans, La., 1906. Durable sideman from Jean Goldkette (1927) to the Nicksieland bands of the forties.

BOSTIC, Earl. ALTO SAXOPHONE. B. Tulsa, Okla., 1913. A screecher with a style, Bostic emerged from many bands to become a rhythm and blues success in the forties and fifties.

BRADLEY, Will. TROMBONE. B. Newton, N.J., 1912. A mixture of backgrounds: Red Nichols, studios, his own band with Ray McKinley (1939-42). A mixture of styles: barrelhouse, suave, almost anything called for on his horn. Will is also a composer in the twelve-tone idiom, and in it at a considerable remove from jazz.

BRADLEY, William Ackerson. DRUMS. B. New York, N.Y., 1938. Trombonist Will's son and thoroughly adept in the modern small-band style.

BRAFF, Reuben "Ruby." TRUMPET. B. Boston, Mass., 1927. A modern Dixielander with a large sound and the ability to fit into most different kinds of small bands.

BRAUD, Wellman. BASS. B. St. James, La., 1891. Best known for his years with Duke Ellington (1926-35).

BROOKMEYER, Robert. VALVE TROMBONE. B. Kansas City, Kan., 1929. Neat, nimble performer who started as a pianist, developed style and facility at once with Stan Getz (1953) and Gerry Mulligan (1954).

BROONZY, William Lee Conley "Big Bill." BLUES SINGER, GUITAR. B. Scott, Miss., 1893. A veteran of the famous shouting years, the late twenties and early thirties. In recent years a great favorite in Europe.

BROWN, Boyce. ALTO SAXOPHONE. B. Chicago, Ill., 1910. One of the Chicago Dixielanders in the twenties, Brown entered the Servite Order in 1953 (as Brother Matthew), where from time to time he continues to play some jazz.

BROWN, Clifford. TRUMPET. B. Wilmington, Del., 1930; killed in auto accident, 1956, on the Pennsylvania Turnpike. Brilliantly gifted post-bop horn man who made his deepest impact in the fifties with a variety of bands, most notably paired with Max Roach from 1953 until his death. Impeccable technique and richness of tone were among Brownie's several gifts.

BROWN, Lawrence. TROMBONE. B. Lawrence, Kan., 1905. Brought up in California, Lawrence went from Aimee Semple McPherson's temple to various Los Angeles bands, finally joined Duke Ellington, with whom he stayed from 1932 to 1951. Long famous as an elegant ballad soloist fully capable of swinging staccato figures in up-tempo jazz.

BROWN, Pete. ALTO, TENOR SAXOPHONE. B. Baltimore, Md., 1906. Famous for bouncing alto contributions to the swing scene.

BROWN, Raymond Matthews "Ray." BASS. B. Pittsburgh, Pa., 1926. Vital part of some of the first bop bands, later a fixture in various recording groups organized by Norman Granz.

BRUBECK, David W. PIANO. B. Concord, Calif., 1920. Classical background, including composition under Darius Milhaud and Arnold Schönberg, led to experiments in San Francisco in the late 1940s with various chamber jazz groups. After 1954 a remarkable national success, both as pianist and leader of the Brubeck Quartet; for many his is the identifying modern jazz style. His own playing emphasizes original chord structure and a delicate interweaving of piano and alto saxophone (Paul Desmond) solos.

BRUNIES, George. TROMBONE. B. New Orleans, La., 1900. From Papa Laine, the New Orleans Rhythm Kings, and Ted Lewis (1923-35) to a variety of Dixieland bands as trombonist, singer, and wit.

BRYANT, William Stevens "Willie." LEADER. B. New Orleans, La., 1908. Singer and emcee, more recently a disk jockey. Fine picker of men for his 1933-39 band, one of the best of the swing era (among those who passed through: Teddy Wilson, Ben Webster, Benny Carter).

BUCKNER, Milton. PIANO. B. St. Louis, Mo., 1915. "Locked-hands" specialist with Lionel Hampton (off and on from 1941-52) and own bands.

BURKE, Vinny. BASS. B. Newark, N.J., 1921. A modernist recently distinguished as leader of his own small group.

BURNS, Ralph. ARRANGER, PIANO. B. Newton, Mass., 1922. A piano-playing prodigy with a brief New England Conservatory education and a long-lived career as Woody Herman's arranger almost all the time that Woody has worked since 1944. His scoring skills extend as far as a recent transcription for jazz instruments of Moussorgsky's *Pictures at an Exhibition.*

BUSHKIN, Joe. PIANO. B. New York, N.Y., 1916. Dixielander with a lovely touch, best known for his association with Tommy Dorsey in the early forties.

BUTTERFIELD, Billy. TRUMPET. B. Middletown, Ohio, 1917. Bob Crosby's barrel-toned soloist (1937-40) who distinguished himself in and out of big bands and little ones, as a Dixielander with ballad-playing proclivities.

BUTTERFIELD, Don. TUBA. B. Centralia, Wash., 1923. One who has made the tuba really swing in big bands and small, on and off records. Educated at Juilliard.

BYAS, Don. TENOR SAXOPHONE. B. Muskogee, Okla., 1912. Background with Redman, Millinder, Kirk, Basie. Since 1950 a fixture in France. A big-toned Hawkins-like musician particularly skillful in constructing ballad lines.

BYERS, Billy. TROMBONE, ARRANGER. B. Los Angeles, Calif., 1937. Very active in radio, television, and records in the fifties; an arranger of broad modern skills.

BYRD, Donald. TRUMPET. B. Detroit, Mich., 1932. One of the most polished of the new Detroiters, a trumpeter of large skills and originality.

CACERES, Ernie. BARITONE SAXOPHONE. B. Rockport, Texas, 1911. Anchor man for the Dixielanders since the late thirties.

CALLENDER, George "Red." BASS. B. Richmond, Va., 1918. Highly responsible performer in the Blanton tradition; a basic part of the West Coast scene.

CALLOWAY, Cab. SINGER. B. Rochester, N.Y., 1907. The man who made scat singing commercially successful. Through most of the 1940s he led a large band of high jazz quality, with such men as Chu Berry, Dizzy Gillespie and Milt Hinton among its regulars.

CANDOLI, Conte. TRUMPET. B. Mishawaka, Ind., 1927. Slick modern trumpeter with, among others, Stan Kenton and Woody Herman.

CANDOLI, Pete. TRUMPET. B. Mishawaka, Ind., 1923. Woody Herman's high-note specialist (1944-46); later brought his blasting skills to studio bands on the West Coast.

CAREY, Thomas "Papa Mutt." TRUMPET. New Orleans, La., 1891-1948. Kid Ory's quondam trumpeter, a significant part of New

Orleans jazz at home and abroad (Chicago, California, New York).

CARNEY, Harry. BARITONE SAXOPHONE. B. Boston, Mass., 1910. Early on in his career (1926) he joined Duke Ellington, with whom he has remained ever since, the man who first demonstrated the solo potentialities of his instrument in jazz.

CARTER, Bennett Lester "Benny." ALTO SAXOPHONE, TRUMPET, AR-RANGER. B. New York, N.Y., 1907. One of the most versatile and most liberally endowed of jazz musicians. Benny's playing experience includes Fletcher Henderson, Chick Webb, McKinney's Cotton Pickers, Willie Bryant, and a variety of bands of his own in the United States and Europe (1935-38). His most enduring reputation is as an alto man, large of tone, melodic ingenuity, every technical facility.

CARVER, Wayman. FLUTE, ALTO SAXOPHONE. B. Portsmouth, Va., 1905. First introduced the flute into jazz with Chick Webb in the thirties.

CARY, Dick. PIANO, TRUMPET, ALTO HORN. B. Hartford, Conn., 1916. A Dixielander with modern tendencies and several instruments at his command, all well exhibited in recent years with the Bobby Hackett Sextet.

CASEY, Albert. GUITAR. B. Louisville, Ky., 1915. Fats Waller's impressive sidekick (1934-42).

CATLETT, Big Sid. DRUMS. B. Evansville, Ind., 1910; d. Chicago, Ill., 1951. With Benny Carter, McKinney, Fletcher Henderson, Don Redman, Louis Armstrong, Teddy Wilson, in the thirties and forties. Early modernist with extraordinary steadiness of beat and the ability to rise to any jazz occasion.

CELESTIN, Oscar "Papa." CORNET. B. Lafourche, La., 1884; d. New Orleans, La., 1954. Brass-band background led to his own small groups, some of the longest-lived and best known in New Orleans.

CHALOFF, Serge. BARITONE SAXOPHONE. B. Boston, Mass., 1923. One of the first to modernize his instrument (with Georgie Auld in

1945). Important contribution to the Herman band (1947-49). Afterward most of the time in Boston.

CHAMBERS, Paul. BASS. B. Pittsburgh, Pa., 1935. A versatile musician of large technical skills who made a deep impression as rhythm musician and soloist in his work with Miles Davis after 1955.

CHARLES, Teddy. VIBRAPHONE. B. Chicopee Falls, Mass., 1928. Emerged from the bands of others (Benny Goodman, Chubby Jackson, Buddy De Franco, Artie Shaw) to lead own chamber groups of a distinctly experimental flavor contributed by his own scores and those of Juilliard faculty member Hall Overton.

CHITTISON, Herman. PIANO. B. Flemingsburg, Ky., 1909. A Tatum-like technician of high good taste who worked in Europe and Egypt (1932-39).

CHRISTIAN, Charles. GUITAR. B. Dallas, Texas, 1919; d. New York, N.Y., 1942. The founder of the modern guitar and in some ways the most significant of the precursors of bop, Christian developed his style with Benny Goodman from 1939 until late 1941, just before a severe siege with tuberculosis forced his retirement from jazz. He was equally at ease in long single-string lines and well-filled chords and notable always for an even rhythmic line which much influenced the construction of the bop cadence.

CHRISTY, June. SINGER. B. Springfield, Ill., 1925. Anita O'Day's replacement with Stan Kenton (1945) and much like her in her husky modern jazz inflections.

CLARKE, Kenneth Spearman "Kenny." DRUMS. B. Pittsburgh, Pa., 1914. Before the bop bands, which he had so much to do with organizing and directing, Kenny's background included Roy Eldridge, Claude Hopkins, Teddy Hill, Benny Carter, and Red Allen. One of the most skillful of modern drummers, he has had much to do with the development of what might be called a melodic line for the drummer. What he himself can do with such a line can be heard with the Modern Jazz Quartet and dozens of date bands with which he figures as sideman or occasionally as leader.

CLAYTON, Wilbur "Buck." TRUMPET. B. Parsons, Kan., 1911. Count Basie's famous muted soloist (1936-43) and one of the most generously recorded of date musicians, Buck is particularly persuasive in constructing counter-melodies behind such singers as Billie Holiday.

COHN, Al. TENOR SAXOPHONE, ARRANGER. B. Brooklyn, N.Y., 1925. Bands: Georgie Auld, Alvino Rey, Buddy Rich, Woody Herman, Artie Shaw, Elliot Lawrence, from the mid-forties to the mid-fifties. Particularly able both as performer and as arranger, in constructing swinging middle- and up-tempo figures.

COLE, Nat "King." PIANO, SINGER. B. Montgomery, Ala., 1917. To begin with, a jazz pianist of considerable ingenuity in the Hines idiom, leader of his own trio for ten years from 1939 on. Later, more a modern-day crooner than jazz musician.

COLE, William "Cozy." DRUMS. B. East Orange, N.J., 1909. With Willie Bryant (1935-36), Stuff Smith (1936-38), Cab Calloway (1939-42), Louis Armstrong (1940-53). These associations suggest Cozy's versatility and dependability; he is unquestionably one of the topnotch technicians among jazz drummers.

COLEMAN, Bill. TRUMPET. B. Paris, Ky., 1904. One of the important jazz figures in Europe off and on since the mid-thirties.

COLLINS, John. GUITAR. B. Montgomery, Ala., 1913. Quite authoritative modernist.

COLLINS, Lee. TRUMPET. B. New Orleans, La., 1901. One of the most durable and variously able of Dixielanders.

CONDON, Eddie. GUITAR. B. Goodland, Ind., 1904. One of the famous Chicagoans of the 1920s and perhaps even better known as a New Yorker (since 1928). Highly talented organizer, an articulate master of ceremonies, a successful night-club owner, very much a part of jazz since the early twenties.

COOPER, Bob. TENOR SAXOPHONE, OBOE, ENGLISH HORN. B. Pittsburgh, Pa., 1925. For more than a decade a West Coast modernist on the several reeds indicated.

COSTA, Eddie. PIANO. B. Mt. Carmel, Pa., 1930. One of the most imaginative and broadly equipped of modern keyboard artists. Part of New York jazz since 1947, notably with the Sal Salvador Quartet.

COX, Ida. SINGER. B. Knoxville, Tenn., 1889. One of the justly famous blues singers of the twenties and thirties, still capable of an exuberant shout or two in the early forties.

CRAWFORD, James Strickland. DRUMS. B. Memphis, Tenn., 1910. Jimmie Lunceford's founding drummer, still very much alive and kicking.

CRISS, William "Sonny." ALTO SAXOPHONE. B. Memphis, Tenn., 1927. One of the better Parker-influenced altoists.

DAMERON, Tadd. PIANO, ARRANGER. B. Cleveland, Ohio, 1917. One of the first of the scorers of bop for Billy Eckstine, Dizzy Gillespie, etc.

D'AMICO, Henry "Hank." CLARINET. B. Rochester, N.Y., 1915. Swing clarinetist (Red Norvo, Bob Crosby, Tommy Dorsey, others). Later with the studios.

DANKWORTH, Johnny. ALTO SAXOPHONE. B. London, England, 1927. Most prominent of British jazzmen, as performer, arranger, and leader. A modernist much influenced by Charlie Parker and considerably at ease in bop and related jazz.

DAVENPORT, Charles "Cow-Cow." PIANO, SINGER. B. Anniston, Ala., 1894. One of the first of the boogie-woogie pianists.

DAVIS, Miles. TRUMPET. B. Alton, Ill., 1926. A delicate sound characterizes this bopper, leader of experimental groups, always developing and thinking jazz musician.

DAVIS, William S. "Wild Bill." ORGAN. B. Glasgow, Mo., 1918. One of the first to turn the manuals and pedals of the electric organ loose in modern jazz.

DAVISON, William "Wild Bill." CORNET. B. Defiance, Ohio, 1906. Standard equipment in Nicksieland jazz in the forties and fifties.

DE FRANCO, Buddy. CLARINET. B. Camden, N.J., 1923. A musician of many parts, sizable tone, and intellectual curiosity. Best known of his early band associations was Tommy Dorsey, off and on from 1944 to 1948. Since then he has had his own groups, of various sizes and textures, but always provocative musically.

DE PARIS, Sidney. TRUMPET. B. Crawfordsville, Ind., 1905. With McKinney, Don Redman, Benny Carter, and in own combination with brother Wilbur.

DE PARIS, Wilbur. TROMBONE. B. Crawfordsville, Ind., 1900. With Blue Rhythm, Sissle, Benny Carter, Teddy Hill, Armstrong, Ellington. With brother Sidney leader of a band much admired by Dixielanders.

DESMOND, Paul. ALTO SAXOPHONE. B. San Francisco, Calif., 1924. Deft modernist with every sort of thinking and playing skill, who has become as vital a part of the Dave Brubeck Quartet since joining it in 1951 as its leader.

DICKENSON, Vic. TROMBONE. B. Xenia, Ohio, 1906. A barrelhouse musician of great good humor on and off his horn who has played with many bands and never seemed out of place, no matter how different the styles of the surrounding musicians from his own Dixieland qualities.

DODDS, Johnny. CLARINET. B. New Orleans, La., 1892; d. Chicago, Ill., 1940. Louis Armstrong's famous associate in the late twenties; earlier with King Oliver and Kid Ory. A major figure on his instrument in the shaping years of Dixieland.

DODDS, Warren "Baby." DRUMS. B. New Orleans, La., 1898. The drumming opposite number of brother Johnny.

DORHAM, Kenny. TRUMPET. B. Fairfield, Texas, 1924. A bopper with a style of his own, most effective in the middle register.

DORSEY, Jimmy. CLARINET, ALTO SAXOPHONE. B. Shenandoah, Pa., 1904; d. New York, N.Y., 1957. One of the founders of the swing clarinet style; out of a broad background, including Goldkette, Whiteman, and Nichols. A more generously talented jazz musician than his surroundings indicated.

DORSEY, Tommy. TROMBONE. B. Shenandoah, Pa., 1905; d. Greenwich, Conn., 1956. Originally a trumpeter as well as a trombonist, a Dixieland soloist of considerable skill, but best known as the most mellifluous of ballad-playing trombonists. His own bands featured a variety of distinguished soloists and arrangers and styles, but the identifying T. D. style was a heavy two-beat closely related to the Lunceford band, from whom Tommy took arranger Sy Oliver to fashion it for him.

DREW, Kenny. PIANO. B. New York, N.Y., 1928. An agile modernist.

DURHAM, Eddie. ARRANGER, GUITAR, TROMBONE. B. San Marcos, Texas, 1906. An arranger of particular ability who wrote for the Lunceford band and for a while for Count Basie as well.

DUTRAY, Honoré. TROMBONE. New Orleans, La., 1894-1935. Longtime associate of King Oliver; one of the best equipped of the early jazzmen.

DUVIVIER, George. BASS, ARRANGER. B. New York, N.Y., 1920. Much admired and much sought by a variety of modernists both on strings and paper.

EAGER, Allen. TENOR SAXOPHONE. B. New York, N.Y., 1927. Grew up with bop in the mid-forties and was one of the first to make commendable to the younger generation the style of Lester Young. With the bands of Tadd Dameron and Buddy Rich and various small groups, including his own.

ECKSTINE, Billy. SINGER. B. Pittsburgh, Pa., 1914. After a variety of band experience (Earl Hines and his own) and changes of name (originally William Clarence Eckstein), Billy stepped out on his own in 1948 to become one of the most original of modern ballad singers with jazz influence. His 1944-47 band included, in a variety of personnels, most of the important boppers, among them Bird, Dizzy, Fats Navarro, Miles Davis, and Leo Parker, and featured, in addition to Billy's own singing, that of Sarah Vaughan.

EDISON, Harry. TRUMPET. B. Columbus, Ohio, 1915. Harry, best known to his friends as "Sweets," was one of the first of the long-lined trumpeters in his long sojourn with the Basie band (1937-50). In recent years his cadenza-like solos have been a vital part of West Coast jazz.

EDWARDS, Eddie. TROMBONE. B. New Orleans, La., 1891. Durable member of the Original Dixieland Jazz Band who was to be heard right into the early fifties.

ELDRIDGE, Roy. TRUMPET. B. Pittsburgh, Pa., 1911. A kind of one-man compendium of this music, and therefore most appropriately known as "Little Jazz." Early bands included Horace Henderson, McKinney, Teddy Hill (1934-35), Fletcher Henderson (1936). Thereafter he alternated between his own little groups, at home and abroad, and brief bright moments with Gene Krupa (1941, 1949) and Artie Shaw (1944-45). A biting, driving brass man, almost without equal for sheer power from the earliest years of swing to the present, Roy is also a singer with some of the same qualities. Few individuals on any instrument in jazz can match him for staying power, from style to style, from decade to decade. Few who have had such influence have retained so thoroughly their own individuality.

ELLINGTON, Edward Kennedy "Duke." PIANIST, COMPOSER, ARRANGER. B. Washington, D.C., 1899. The Ellington story extends from his high-school demonstration of talent as an artist and early studies as a pianist through ragtime jobs from 1916 until 1922. In that year Duke took the first of several trips to New York, and in 1923 he and Sonny Greer and Arthur Whetsol and Toby Hardwick, among others, settled down as a New York band. They moved from the Kentucky Club to the Cotton, gathered musicians of the quality of Bubber Miley, Tricky Sam, Harry Carney, Johnny Hodges, Barney Bigard, and Cootie Williams, and made themselves by 1932 an organization that could justly be called, on and off records, "Duke Ellington and His Famous Orchestra."

Trips to Europe before and after World War II, Carnegie Hall performances (from January 1943 on), and a vast number of recordings of all kinds by every sort of combination of Ellington musicians have assured Duke and his associates of the single most important position among bands thus far in the history of jazz. For most Ellington fanciers the most significant period in the band's history stretched from 1939 to 1942, when Jimmy Blanton played the bass, Ben Webster the tenor saxophone, Ray Nance violin and trumpet, and Billy Strayhorn first began to add his scores to Ellington's to build that extraordinary library altogether without equal in this music. It was for that band that Duke composed what is still the most substantial of his large-scale works, *Black, Brown and Beige.*

ELLIOTT, Don. MELLOPHONE, TRUMPET, VIBRAPHONE. B. Somerville, N.J., 1926. A modernist outstanding for his versatility, Don's emergence as a musician with his own identity dates from the early fifties, when more and more he began to lead his own small bands.

ELMAN, Ziggy. TRUMPET. B. Philadelphia, Pa., 1914. With Benny Goodman (1936-40) he established a style close to that of Harry James, with its own decorative edges borrowed from a music most generally associated with Jewish weddings.

ERWIN, George "Peewee." TRUMPET. B. Falls City, Neb., 1913. A thoroughly reliable sideman in the late twenties and thirties with bands of the quality of Isham Jones, Ray Noble, Benny Goodman, Tommy Dorsey; later and right up to the present a fluent Dixielander.

EVANS, Gil. ARRANGER. B. Toronto, Ontario, 1912. With Claude Thornhill (1941-48), Gil showed an impressive versatility. Especially important for his instrumental contribution, as thinker, composer, and arranger for the Miles Davis Capitol band.

EVANS, Herschel. TENOR SAXOPHONE. B. Denton, Texas, 1909; d. New York, N.Y., 1939. Perhaps the most persuasive of all the ballad-playing tenor men in the Hawkins tradition, Herschel was the famous tenor soloist who alternated with Lester Young in the Count Basie band from 1936 to early 1939.

FARLOW, Tal. GUITAR. B. Greensboro, N.C., 1921. The classical small-group modern guitarist (Red Norvo, Artie Shaw's Gramercy Five, his own trio).

FARMER, Art. TRUMPET. B. Council Bluffs, Iowa, 1928. One of the most broadly experienced and gifted of late boppers.

FAZOLA, Irving. CLARINET. New Orleans, La., 1912-49. A lovely tone marked Faz's work, especially with the Bob Crosby band (1938-40). Few clarinetists showed so well the indebtedness of the swing style to Dixieland; few made both shine so brightly.

FERGUSON, Maynard. TRUMPET. B. Verdun, Quebec, 1928. A high-note specialist with Kenton and others, who in 1956 settled down to leading a band of high jazz quality.

FISHKIN, Arnold. BASS. B. Bayonne, N.J., 1919. After every sort of band experience, Arnold became for a few years (1946-50) Lennie Tristano's redoubtable bass player, capable of all sorts of demanding rhythmic duties in a demanding modern school. More recently a studio musician.

FITZGERALD, Ella. SINGER. B. Newport News, Va., 1918. Chick Webb's discovery (1934) and the equal of that great jazzman in natural vitality and native musicianship. Apart from the unmistakable individuality of her sound, Ella knows no equal in jazz singing for warmth and openness of tone, and the ability at the same time to match the most tender inflections and a swinging beat. Notable too as a scat singer, she was a distinguished performer in all her years with Chick (1934-39), as she has been ever since, on her own, one of the handful of masters of jazz singing.

FONTANA, Carl. TROMBONE. B. Monroe, La., 1928. Big tone, bouncing beat, modern style identify Carl's work, particularly with Woody Herman from 1950 to 1952 and since late 1956 with Kai Winding's four-trombone septet.

FOSTER, George "Pops." BASS. B. McCall, La., 1892. A fixture for years with Luis Russell and Louis Armstrong (the two engagements reaching from 1929 to 1940), and afterward as before an important part of jazz patterned after early New Orleans performances.

FREEMAN, Lawrence "Bud." TENOR SAXOPHONE. B. Chicago, Ill., 1906. The Austin High School gang's star saxophonist; the man who made the tenor acceptable to Dixielanders; the long-lined tenor man who contributed his bit to the making of modern jazz.

FREEMAN, Russ. PIANO. B. Chicago, Ill., 1926. A performer of effective, punchy little figures with the West Coast jazzmen of the late forties and early fifties.

GALBRAITH, Barry. GUITAR. B. Pittsburgh, Pa., 1919. One of the favorite rhythm-section performers of the moderns.

GARNER, Erroll. PIANO. B. Pittsburgh, Pa., 1921. The bounciest of modern pianists, who has effected what is for many a most intriguing combination of stride-style piano and many of the devices of French Impressionist writing for the keyboard—all of it self-taught. His rise was simultaneous with that of bop, with whose musicians he has often had very close associations.

GEE, Matthew, Jr. TROMBONE. B. Houston, Texas, 1921. A remarkably facile trombonist after the fashion of bopper J. J. Johnson. Among his bands: Gillespie, Basie, Jacquet.

GETZ, Stanley. TENOR SAXOPHONE. B. Philadelphia, Pa., 1927. The background of "The Sound," as Stan has appropriately been called, is, in his own words, a "stomping" one. It includes, starting at the age of sixteen, stints with the bands of Jack Teagarden, Bob Chester, Stan Kenton, Jimmy Dorsey, and Benny Goodman. He did not achieve his delicate style, his lovely sonorities, really, until joining the Woody Herman band in 1947, to become one of the famous Four Brothers (the others: Zoot Sims, Serge Chaloff, Herbie Steward). In recent years, Stan has been the definitive "cool" saxophonist and, when in full control of his own resources, a musician of some depth.

GIBBS, Terry. VIBRAPHONE. B. Brooklyn, N.Y., 1924. One of the most intense of modern vibists; another modernist who came into his own with Woody Herman (1948-49), before leaving to lead his own small groups. Has abiding quality, rhythmic vitality.

GILLESPIE, John Birks "Dizzy." TRUMPET, ARRANGER. B. Cheraw, S.C., 1917. Dizzy's background includes most of the brass instruments and early playing experience at school as well as gigging around Philadelphia. An indefatigable sitter-in in New York sessions in the early forties (when he was working with Cab Calloway, Lucky Millinder, Earl Hines, and others), he was the other half of the Gillespie-Parker tandem who probably should be credited with originating bop, or at least bringing it to a boil. Few trumpeters can match Dizzy for ease on his instrument and the articulateness with which he can bring the most fanciful of cadences to precise statement on the trumpet or, through his scores, on other men's horns. A certain nervous agility has always characterized his playing and his writing, along with a broad sense of humor that upon occasion has found effective musical form. In 1957 his big band was one of the best in jazz.

GIUFFRE, Jimmy. CLARINET, TENOR SAXOPHONE, BARITONE SAXOPHONE, ARRANGER. B. Dallas, Texas, 1921. Many bands: Boyd Raeburn, Jimmy Dorsey, Buddy Rich, Woody Herman, etc.; several instruments, and a variety of composing and playing modes, the most recent of which has been a contrapuntal style close to the twelve-tone school. In recent years, too, Jimmy has shown a great interest in rhythmic experiments in his writing.

GLENN, Tyree. TROMBONE, VIBRAPHONE. B. Corsicana, Texas, 1912. This fluent trombonist came into his own with Cab Calloway (1940-46), then after a trip to Europe with Don Redman was with Duke Ellington (until 1951). Later a studio musician.

GOLDKETTE, Jean. PIANO, LEADER. B. Valenciennes, France, 1899. An international background, including early years in Greece and Russia, led to the United States, where in the early twenties Goldkette led a band which employed a remarkably large number of jazz musicians, among them Bix Beiderbecke, Eddie Lang,

Joe Venuti, Frankie Trumbauer, the Dorseys, Jimmy McPartland, etc.

GONSALVES, Paul. TENOR SAXOPHONE. B. Boston, Mass., 1920. An interesting combination of Hawkins and Young influences characterized Paul's work with Basie, Gillespie, and Ellington in the late forties and early fifties.

GONZALES, Babs. SINGER. B. Newark, N.J., 1919. As much as anybody the founder of bop scat singing; with his own vocal group in the late forties.

GOODMAN, Benny. CLARINET. B. Chicago, Ill., 1909. Most famous of jazz clarinetists and in some ways the most generously gifted. From his childhood a prodigious performer, who made his way into jazz in his teens with Ben Pollack, whom he left after some years in 1929 to gig around New York and work in the studios, eventually (1934) to form his own group, which in 1936 made itself the center of the newly established swing epoch. A detailed list of the musicians of quality who have passed through Benny's bands before and after the retirements of recent years would make a small appendix to this book in itself. Suffice it to say here that few bands swung as consistently as Benny's in the late thirties and early forties; that few leaders did as much to find audiences for soloists of a half-dozen different related schools; that few did as much to break down color lines in jazz; that few have demonstrated so unmistakably the classical nature of that refined Dixieland which was swing. For further details see Chapter 1.

GORDON, Bob. BARITONE SAXOPHONE. B. St. Louis, Mo., 1928; killed in an automobile accident in California, 1955. In the few years before his death in which Bob Gordon was more and more featured as a soloist and leader on records, he showed himself more and more a thinking musician with a rich tone, a melodic resourcefulness, and an urge to experiment.

GORDON, Dexter. TENOR SAXOPHONE. B. Los Angeles, Calif., 1923. If one of the most honking, also one of the most booting of bop tenor men. Now once again a West Coaster.

GOWANS, Brad. TROMBONE, CLARINET. B. Billerica, Mass., 1903; d. Los Angeles, Calif., 1954. A variously able musician much influenced by Original Dixieland musicians Larry Shields and Eddie Edwards, and closely associated with the Nicksieland musicians in New York.

GOZZO, Conrad. TRUMPET. B. New Britain, Conn., 1922. A sideman with an astonishing breath and breadth. Few lead men in jazz have been able so to spark a whole section to performances of the highest jazz quality. For all of this Goz is not himself a conspicuous soloist.

GRAETTINGER, Robert. ARRANGER. B. Ontario, Calif., 1923. A provocative composer of works closely related to the twelve-tone school for Stan Kenton.

GRAAS, John. FRENCH HORN, ARRANGER, COMPOSER. B. Dubuque, Iowa, 1924. In the early fifties a vital part of West Coast jazz, giving his instrument, in his own scores and those of others, a warm and flexible voice.

GRAY, Wardell. TENOR SAXOPHONE. B. Oklahoma City, Okla., 1921; d. Las Vegas, Nev., 1955. Another of the driving swingers of the bop school, closely related to Lester Young.

GREEN, Bennie. TROMBONE. B. Chicago, Ill., 1923. Another dexterous trombonist of the bop persuasion, Bennie first achieved fame with Charlie Ventura in the late forties. Later, after several other attachments, he became a leader on his own.

GREEN, Charlie "Big." TROMBONE. New Orleans, La., 1900-35. Fletcher Henderson's barrel-toned barrelhouse trombonist (1923-27). Among his many effective record appearances were several swinging contributions to Bessie Smith performances.

GREEN, Urbie. TROMBONE. B. Mobile, Ala., 1926. After a variety of bands, Urbie achieved something like star status with Woody Herman (1950-52), showing himself a fluent modern musician, but not at all doctrinaire. His versatility made him a natural studio man.

GREENE, Freddy. GUITAR. B. Charleston, S.C., 1911. Freddy moved from a Greenwich Village job to Count Basie's band in early 1937, to remain for Count and for jazz one of the steadiest of guitarists, no soloist, but a rock in the rhythm section.

GREER, William Alexander "Sonny." DRUMS. B. Long Branch, N.J., 1903. The closest of associates of Duke Ellington from 1919 until 1951, a drummer of parts—more than any normal half dozen, i.e., chimes, gourds, etc. A personality and, in both his playing and speaking roles, a central performer in the Ellington drama. In recent years he has played in and around New York with a variety of Ellingtonish and Dizzyish small bands.

GRIMES, Lloyd "Tiny." GUITAR. B. Newport News, Va., 1915. One of the grooviest of swing guitarists, a vital part of the Art Tatum Trio, and at least in the early days a friend of bop and boppers.

GRYCE, Gigi. ALTO SAXOPHONE, FLUTE, ARRANGER. B. Pensacola, Fla, 1927. A New England background led Gigi to Paris (1952), where he studied as a Fulbright scholar. In New York in the last few years, one of the important arrangers for the second generation of boppers and some of the first as well.

GUARNIERI, Johnny. PIANO. B. New York, N.Y., 1917. By taste a stride-stylist closely related to Fats Waller, but by technique capable of almost every keyboard style of the swing years and several of those which followed. Johnny's greatest fame came with Benny Goodman (1939-40) and Artie Shaw (1940-41).

GULDA, Friedrich. PIANO. B. Vienna, Austria, 1930. A skilled concert artist in the classical tradition who plays jazz—in a strictly modern groove—persuasively.

GULLIN, Lars. BARITONE SAXOPHONE. B. Sweden, 1928. An excellently educated musician and one of the most impressive of the Swedish boppers.

GUY, Joe. TRUMPET. B. Birmingham, Ala., 1920. A variety of musical associations can be heard in Joe's versatile performances, the most enduring in recent years being that with bop.

HACKETT, Bobby. CORNET, TRUMPET, GUITAR. B. Providence, R.I., 1915. A traditionalist particularly persuasive in his languorous ballad lines and as such, despite firm Dixieland associations, pleasing to musicians and fans of half a dozen other more modern schools. His playing experience includes almost every sort of combination of instruments, most frequently small jazz groups, most notably for the public at large with Horace Heidt (1939-40), Glenn Miller (1941-42), Glen Gray (1944-46).

HAGGART, Bob. BASS. B. New York, N.Y., 1914. Bob Crosby's reliable plucker, whistler, and arranger (1935-42)—with records under Crosby's aegis long afterward.

HAIG, Al. PIANO. B. Newark, N.J., 1923. A bopper with a background (Charlie Barnet, Jimmy Dorsey), with a lovely touch and the most direct of playing associations with Charlie Parker, Stan Getz, and most recently Chet Baker.

HALL, Edmond. CLARINET. B. New Orleans, La., 1901. A most durable musician whose career extends from various groups in his hometown to bands as different from one another as Claude Hopkins, Lucky Millinder, Red Allen, Teddy Wilson, and Eddie Condon, in the two and a half decades that he has been playing in New York (from 1930 on). His style is Dixieland *cum* swing.

HALLBERG, Bengt. PIANO. B. Göteburg, Sweden, 1932. A superbly trained musician, fleet of finger, gifted with an exquisite touch and considerable melodic resources.

HAMILTON, Chico. DRUMS. B. Los Angeles, Calif., 1921. A variety of West Coast playing experiences led Chico to the Gerry Mulligan Quartet in 1952, later (1956) to form his own quintet, combining saxophone and flute (doubled by Buddy Collette), guitar, bass, cello, and drums.

HAMILTON, Jimmy. CLARINET. B. Dillon, S.C., 1917. Classically trained, big of tone, a fine representative of his instrument with Teddy Wilson (1939-41), Barney Bigard (1941-42), and Duke Ellington (from 1942 on).

HAMPTON, Lionel. VIBRAPHONE, DRUMS. B. Louisville, Ky., 1913.

Lionel made his first great impact—and "impact" is the word—in California in the late twenties, leading to his work with Louis Armstrong in 1930. In 1936 Benny Goodman's trio was increased to quartet size to include Lionel on vibes. In 1940 the Hampton date records on Victor brought together all sorts of interesting new music and musicians; that year, too, he formed his own orchestra, which achieved its greatest success in the midforties (and ever since) as a loud but well-disciplined vaudeville outfit that could be sure to drive all sorts of audiences to a frenzy approaching exhaustion.

HANDY, George. PIANO, ARRANGER. B. Brooklyn, N.Y., 1920. Classically educated, brilliantly experimental in his writing for Boyd Raeburn (1943-46).

HARDWICK, Otto "Toby." ALTO SAXOPHONE. B. Washington, D.C., 1904. Close friend and close musical associate of Duke Ellington from 1918 to 1928 and again from 1932 to 1945. A rich, sinuous, unmistakably individual alto and soprano sax sound characterizes his contributions as leader of the section and soloist in a large number of tours with Ellington.

HARRIS, Bill. TROMBONE. B. Philadelphia, Pa., 1916. After gigs at home and work in New York and elsewhere with Bob Chester and Benny Goodman, Bill brought his curious amalgam of Dixieland and modern trombone styles to bear upon the striking Woody Herman band of 1944-46, an organization which is unthinkable without his rich, burly contribution. In recent years a small-band musician and then with Woody again in 1957.

HARRISON, Jimmy. TROMBONE. B. Louisville, Ky., 1900; d. New York, N.Y., 1931. One of the early giants of jazz with Fletcher Henderson (1926-31) and other bands in New York, most important of them Chick Webb at the very end of Harrison's life. Only snatches of his melodically fluent style can be heard on records, but his influence in the construction of the playing personalities of such disparate musicians as Jack Teagarden, Benny Morton, and Dickie Wells was central.

HART, Clyde. PIANO. B. Baltimore, Md., 1910; d. New York, N.Y., 1945. A small-band pianist of distinction in the late thirties, a significant contributor to the early bop sessions.

HASSELGARD, Stan. CLARINET. B. Bollnäs, Sweden, 1922; d. in an automobile accident in Illinois, 1948. Stan arrived in the United States in 1947, worked briefly with Benny Goodman, showed himself a modernist of considerable ingenuity in his brief career in this country.

HAWES, Hampton. PIANO. B. Los Angeles, Calif., 1928. A successful West Coast modernist with and without his own trio.

HAWKINS, Coleman. TENOR SAXOPHONE. B. St. Joseph, Mo., 1904. Hawk (also known to friends as "Bean"), made the tenor saxophone come alive in jazz, recommending it to thousands the world over because of the sweep of his solos, the gargantuan tone (perhaps not unrelated to his early lessons on the cello), his ingenious alternations of the progressions of familiar tunes. His indelible associations in jazz are those with Fletcher Henderson (1923-34), with jazz in Europe (1934-39), with his own bands in this country (after 1939). He showed a considerable sympathy for the early bop performances and in fact recorded several times with Dizzy and others of the first generation of boppers. In later years his work has been somewhat more conventional but never less than appealing in its careful construction and great warmth.

HEATH, Percy. BASS. B. Wilmington, N.C., 1923. A particularly musicianlike bopper, today best known for his work (since 1954) with the Modern Jazz Quartet.

HEFTI, Neal. TRUMPET, ARRANGER. B. Hastings, Neb., 1922. One of those who helped put together the conspicuously fresh library of the Woody Herman band (1944-46 edition). Later a slick arranger for Count Basie and his own bands. More and more conventional as a scripter but never entirely lacking in modern influences and interest.

HENDERSON, Fletcher. PIANO, ARRANGER. B. Cuthbert, Ga., 1898;

d. New York, N.Y., 1952. The substance of the achievement of this mild-mannered, broadly talented musician can be found in the chronicle which makes up Chapter 1. Here it is worth adding that "Smack" started out to be a chemist at Atlanta University and never altogether lost the appearance of a scholar. In his sponsorship of musicians and his influence upon jazz, both in his own bands and through the work he did for Benny Goodman, he stands beside Ellington, Goodman, Basie, Gillespie, and Herman as one of the half-dozen most important leaders in the history of this music.

HENDERSON, Horace. PIANO. B. Cuthbert, Ga., 1904. Fletcher's brother, an arranger of like interests and like skills; a sometime band leader, mostly for recordings, but in recent years a sort of territory band leader working out of Chicago.

HERMAN, Woody. CLARINET, ALTO SAXOPHONE, SINGER. B. Milwaukee, Wis., 1913. A vastly accomplished showman whose vaudeville experience reaches back to the tender age of six. When the Isham Jones band was dissolved in 1936, Woody and the more important members of the organization formed a cooperative organization, emphasizing the blues and Dixieland styles. In the forties Woody's tastes became more and more modern until, with the 1944 band, he declared himself a modernist without any reservations. Thereafter he has consistently sponsored music and musicians variously experimental but thoroughly up to date in time and general conception. As an instrumentalist Woody is very close to sounds and styles associated with swing and Dixieland. As a singer, he is perhaps more closely related to the style of Red McKenzie, with a carefully controlled vibrato, a most musicianly sense of phrase, and a very pleasing baritone voice. As a leader he has always been capable of inspiring musicians to peak performance and audiences to the warmest appreciation of his musicians.

HIGGINBOTHAM, J. C. TROMBONE. B. Atlanta, Ga., 1906. After beginnings with Chick Webb, Fletcher Henderson, Mills Blue Rhythm, and Louis Armstrong, Higgy made his most lasting impression with the Red Allen band through the forties. A barrel-house trombonist of tremendous power, Higginbotham was also capable upon occasion of well-organized ballad lines perhaps constructed after the fashion of Jimmy Harrison, with whom he worked for a while in his early years.

HILL, Bertha "Chippie." SINGER. B. Charleston, S.C., 1905; d. New York, N.Y., 1950. One of the best-accompanied, biggest toned, most swinging blues singers of the twenties, still very much worth listening to in comeback appearances in the late forties.

HILL, Teddy. LEADER. B. Birmingham, Ala., 1909. A shrewd selector of musicians (Chu Berry, Roy Eldridge, Dickie Wells, Dizzy Gillespie, among others); a significant part of the swing era in Harlem; more or less the sponsor of bop at Minton's.

HINES, Earl "Fatha." PIANO. B. Duquesne, Pa., 1905. Of all the pianists of jazz, the most widely influential and in some ways the most generously gifted, with a stretch in time as strikingly long as his reach across the piano keys with his great, expansive hands. Founder not only of modern piano style but of almost every other from the early twenties, when he established himself in Chicago, first with Carroll Dickerson, then with Jimmie Noone and Louis Armstrong, finally with his own band at the Grand Terrace for some twenty years (1928-48). At no point in his career has he ever been capable of an altogether sloppy performance; his precise muscular fingering ("trumpet-style piano," it has been called) of single-note lines, and his tremolos—his forceful chording in the left hand—together formed the base of the styles of Teddy Wilson, Art Tatum, and all the others who came afterward. Although his appearances in recent years with Louis Armstrong have seemed to associate him with an earlier period of jazz than swing or the postwar styles, it would be unfair to class Hines as anything less than universal in range and interest and influence.

HINTON, Milton. BASS. B. Vicksburg, Miss., 1910. A brilliantly gifted musician with a natural tone large enough to match his eighteenth-century instrument, Milton has come into his own since

1951, after half a dozen years with Cab Calloway and as many before with various Chicago groups.

HIPP, Jutta. PIANO. B. Leipzig, Germany, 1925. Most impressive of the postwar German pianists, strictly modern in her playing at home and abroad (New York after late 1955).

HODGES, Johnny. ALTO SAXOPHONE. B. Cambridge, Mass., 1906. Duke Ellington's resourceful all-around altoist from 1928 on (he led his own small band from 1951 to 1955). Particularly notable for sinuous sliding lines and punchy little jazz figures, Johnny has been the insinuating voice of Ellington in every sort of soft and slow and melodic music.

HOLIDAY, Billie. SINGER. B. Baltimore, Md., 1915. The definitive modern jazz singer, after whom most significant jazz singing styles since swing have been fashioned. Some of the distinction comes in her scoops of pitch, some in her husky, coarse-grained sound, and a good deal more in the nuances she gives both verbal and musical phrase. Her band experience includes brief excursions with Artie Shaw and Count Basie and every sort of recording outfit, most notably those led by Teddy Wilson (1935-39).

HOLLAND, Peanuts. TRUMPET. B. Norfolk, Va., 1910. An effusive playing and singing personality who made his deepest impression with Charlie Barnet (1941-46).

HOLMAN, Bill. TENOR SAXOPHONE, ARRANGER. B. Olive, Calif., 1927. Kenton's facile modern jazz arranger off and on since 1952.

HOPKINS, Claude. PIANO. B. Washington, D.C., 1903. A well-educated musician, most significant in jazz as a leader who at one time or another has employed such musicians as Jabbo Smith on trumpet (his most famous sideman), Vic Dickensen, and Edmond Hall.

HORNE, Lena. SINGER. B. Brooklyn, N.Y., 1917. A versatile singer capable of persuasive jazz lines, to which she seems to need to return again and again after flurries as a pop singer, actress, and motion-picture star.

HUCKO, Peanuts. CLARINET. B. Syracuse, N.Y., 1918. Capable reed man of mixed swing and Dixieland proclivities.

HUG, Armand. PIANO. B. New Orleans, La., 1910. One of the most imaginative of modern Dixieland keyboard artists.

HUMES, Helen. SINGER. B. Louisville, Ky., 1913. For at least a half-dozen years (four with Basie, 1938-42, and several thereafter), Helen sang with remarkable loveliness of tone and delicacy of phrase. Later, perhaps because of economic exigencies, a more ordinary and much louder blues singer.

HUNTER, Alberta. SINGER. B. Memphis, Tenn., 1897. Perhaps the most influential of all American blues singers in Europe; distinguished in the States for the quality of her jazz accompanists, among them Fletcher Henderson, Louis Armstrong, Fats Waller.

IGOE, Sonny. DRUMS. B. Jersey City, N.J., 1923. Flexible modernist, much experienced with a variety of bands, including a particularly effective two years with Woody Herman (1950-52).

IRVIS, Charlie. TROMBONE. New York, N.Y., 1899-1939. Founder of the growl trombone slot with Duke Ellington (1924-26); later a New York fixture in the years up to and including most of the swing era.

ISOLA, Frank. DRUMS. B. Detroit, Mich., 1925. Gifted with a keyboard-like light touch, well demonstrated in stints with Stan Getz and Gerry Mulligan in the fifties.

JACKSON, Chubby. BASS. B. New York, N.Y., 1918. After generous band experience tailored to fit his outsize figure, he was a vital part of the spirit, the beat, and the showmanship of the Woody Herman band from 1943-46 and several times since. A great enthusiast for and inspirer of much vital modern jazz, including several groups he has led himself.

JACKSON, Mahalia. SINGER. B. New Orleans, La., 1911. A blues singer gifted with a large, true voice and a personality that moved easily into swinging religious music, that genre best known as "gospel singing." A considerable and justified success was hers in the mid-fifties, on records and radio.

JACKSON, Milton "Bags." VIBRAPHONE. B. Detroit, Mich., 1923. In idea, at least, one of the most subtle of vibists, an eloquent member of the Gillespie band and various other bop groups with which he worked from the mid-forties until joining the Modern Jazz Quartet in 1953, in which he has occupied a most impressive corner.

JACKSON, Quentin. TROMBONE. B. Springfield, Ohio, 1909. A broad background led to his replacing Tricky Sam in 1948 as growler-in-ordinary for Ellington.

JACKSON, Tony. PIANO. B. New Orleans, La., 1876; d. Chicago, Ill., 1921. One of the most influential of the ragtime pianists, both as a performer and composer.

JAFFE, Nat. PIANO. New York, N.Y., 1918-45. Early education in Berlin; later schooling on Fifty-second Street. A brilliant accompanist for Billie Holiday, among others, and one of the first, in the early forties, to make effective use of all the developing modern styles on the keyboard.

JAMES, Harry. TRUMPET. B. Albany, Ga., 1916. Tutored by his father, a circus trumpeter of considerable brass-band skill, Harry became one of the giant names in jazz as a result of his years with Benny Goodman (1936-39) and his own bands thereafter.

JASPAR, Bobby. TENOR SAXOPHONE. B. Liège, Belgium, 1926. A very recent émigré to the United States (mid-1956); perhaps the most welcome reed man to cross the Atlantic since Coleman Hawkins went the other way. Bobby specializes in cool, crafty, tightly constructed solos.

JEFFERSON, Hilton. ALTO SAXOPHONE. B. Danbury, Conn., 1903. A superb lead with Fletcher Henderson, Cab Calloway (1940-51), Duke Ellington, and others.

JENKINS, Freddy "Posey." TRUMPET. B. New York, N.Y., 1906. Duke

Ellington's major showman in the formative years (1928-34) who had to retire because of illness.

JENNEY, Jack. TROMBONE. B. Mason City, Iowa, 1910; d. Los Angeles, Calif., 1945. One of the finest of ballad-playing jazz musicians, particularly skillful in matching a rich tone and a well-controlled vibrato to the melodic phrases at hand, in work with his own band, Artie Shaw's, and others.

JOHNSON, Budd. TENOR SAXOPHONE. B. Dallas, Texas, 1910. A mainstay with Earl Hines from 1934 till 1942 and a significant performer in the early years of bop with small bands on Fifty-second Street and Billy Eckstine.

JOHNSON, Gus. DRUMS. B. Tyler, Texas, 1913. Manufacturer of a powerful beat for Jay McShann in the early forties and for Count Basie in the early fifties.

JOHNSON, James Louis "J. J." TROMBONE. B. Indianapolis, Ind., 1924. Bop's premiere slide man, well enough equipped technically to handle the rich, sometimes complex products of his imagination. For two years (1954-56) partner with Kai Winding in an unusual band featuring two trombone-playing leaders.

JOHNSON, James Price. PIANO. B. New Brunswick, N.J., 1891; d. New York, N.Y., 1955. Classically trained instructor of Fats Waller and many others who did not work directly with him, James P. had much to do with expanding keyboard resources in jazz to include the most useful of ragtime and classical phrases and techniques.

JOHNSON, Keg. TROMBONE. B. Dallas, Texas, 1908. A significant performer with Benny Carter, Fletcher Henderson, and Cab Calloway in the years just before and all through those of swing.

JOHNSON, Osie. DRUMS. B. Washington, D.C., 1923. A drummer with a fine feeling for the modern melodic line and a rich set of sounds. Well tutored in all sorts of bands, most importantly with Earl Hines's small group in 1952-53.

JOHNSON, Pete. PIANO. B. Kansas City, Mo., 1904. Swinging boogie-woogie musician closely associated for many years with the blues singer Joe Turner, and later well known for his appearances with Albert Ammons and Meade Lux Lewis in b.w. marathons.

JOHNSON, William Gary "Bunk." CORNET, TRUMPET. B. New Orleans, La., 1879; d. New Iberia, La., 1949. A performer whose precise importance in the early history of jazz has never satisfactorily been established, but certainly one much heard on and off in New Orleans until the early 1930s. Later (1938) rediscovered by admirers of New Orleans jazz who persuaded him, five years later, to emerge from retirement and make a series of appearances on the two Coasts; these moved some deeply because of an ostensible loveliness of tone and melodic invention, and bothered or annoyed others who could find no such virtues in his playing.

JOLLY, Pete. PIANO, ACCORDION. B. New Haven, Conn., 1932. An able modern pianist and an even better accordionist of some melodic freshness.

JONES, Hank. PIANO. B. Pontiac, Mich., 1918. Fine all-around modern pianist, particularly skillful in accompanying such singers as Billy Eckstine and Ella Fitzgerald.

JONES, Jimmy. PIANO. B. Chicago, Ill., 1918. Softest voiced of keyboard artists, particularly persuasive as an accompanist (he has been Sarah Vaughan's from 1947 to the present, with two years off because of illness, 1952-54). His identifying characteristic: unusual, well-filled chords, quietly enunciated.

JONES, Jonah. TRUMPET. B. Louisville, Ky., 1909. A vibrant personality with a variety of bands: Horace Henderson, Lunceford, Stuff Smith, Fletcher Henderson, Cab Calloway (1941-52).

JONES, Jonathan "Jo." DRUMS. B. Chicago, Ill., 1911. Count Basie's indefatigable drummer (1936-48); thereafter a wandering jazzman much heard with small groups on and off records. A deft man with the high hats and the cymbals, and, particularly, the top cymbal.

JONES, Quincy, Jr. TRUMPET, PIANO, ARRANGER. B. Chicago, Ill., 1933. Well-instructed, well-experienced (Lionel Hampton, Ray Anthony,

Dizzy Gillespie) performer and arranger, much in demand by small group leaders, especially for record sessions.

JONES, Richard "Myknee." PIANO. B. New Orleans, La., 1899; d. Chicago, Ill., 1945. An important figure in Storyville houses; a minor figure in the jazz that came afterward, beloved of many admirers of early jazz.

JONES, Thad. TRUMPET. B. Pontiac, Mich., 1923. Perhaps the most "trumpetistic" of modern trumpeters, a brilliant performer on records and (when heard) with Count Basie since 1954. Brother of pianist Hank and drummer Elvin.

JORDAN, Duke. PIANO. B. Brooklyn, N.Y., 1922. An early bop pianist, a swinging one, still very much a part of jazz.

JORDAN, Louis, ALTO SAXOPHONE, SINGER. B. Brinkley, Ark., 1908. A witty musician whose personality has helped sell jazz to many not ordinarily interested in this music since 1938, when he organized his own small group, the Tympany Five. In recent years illness has cut down the number of his performances.

JORDAN, Taft. TRUMPET, SINGER. B. Florence, S.C., 1915. Featured trumpeter and singer with Chick Webb (and Ella Fitzgerald) from 1933 to 1942; later with Duke Ellington (1943-47). An able, gravel-throated singer and simple, punchy trumpeter in the Louis Armstrong fashion.

KAHN, Norman "Tiny." DRUMS, ARRANGER. New York, N.Y., 1924-53. A remarkably talented drummer whose playing showed some of the same skill in carrying out long lines that his fine manuscript did. Deeply admired and much imitated by a variety of modern musicians, especially arrangers.

KAMINSKY, Max. TRUMPET. B. Brockton, Mass., 1908. A Dixielander with a beat, melodic resourcefulness, and all sorts of experience ranging from Red Nichols to the bands of Tommy Dorsey, Artie Shaw, and the various Nicksieland groups.

KATZ, Dick. PIANO, ARRANGER. B. Baltimore, Md., 1924. Tony Scott's skillful pianist and arranger since 1952.

KATZ, Fred. CELLO, PIANO, ARRANGER. B. Brooklyn, N.Y., 1919. A significant part of modern jazz since taking up the cello to fill out the Chico Hamilton Quintet in late 1955.

KENNEY, Beverly. SINGER. B. Harrison, N.J., 1932. An able, husky-voiced new arrival in jazz, much influenced by Billie Holiday.

KENTON, Stanley Newcomb. PIANO, ARRANGER. B. Wichita, Kan., 1912. One of the largest figures in jazz in many ways. A gusty, enthusiastic man who has carried much of modern jazz along with him to huge audiences since his band (founded at Balboa Beach, Calif., 1941) became thoroughly attuned to a broadly experimental modernity in the mid-forties. His most significant arrangers in the modern years have been Pete Rugolo, who supplied Kenton with some of his most successful riffy pieces; Bob Graettinger, a composer much influenced by twelve-tone procedures; and a variety of swinging, up-to-date modernists, most important of whom has been Bill Holman. No one soloist stands out among the many talents who have passed through the Kenton band, but perhaps the most significant have been Kai Winding, Milt Bernhart (trombones), Shorty Rogers (trumpet), Art Pepper, Bud Shank, Lee Konitz, Lennie Niehaus (altos), Bob Cooper, Bill Perkins (tenors), Laurindo Almeida (guitar), Shelly Manne (drums).

KEPPARD, Freddie. TRUMPET. B. New Orleans, La., 1883; d. Chicago, Ill., 1932. Much admired by those who played alongside him or listened to him in New Orleans before the First World War and Chicago during and just after it, Keppard achieved his greatest fame for his beat.

KERSEY, Kenny. PIANO. B. Harrow, Ontario, 1916. A distinguished small-band pianist particularly well known in the swing years.

KESSEL, Barney. GUITAR. B. Muskogee, Okla., 1923. A brilliant single-string performer who, in tone and beat, reminds one all at once of a classical lutanist and Charlie Christian. An ornament of West Coast jazz.

KILLIAN, Albert. TRUMPET. B. Birmingham, Ala., 1916; d. Los Angeles, Calif., 1950. Remarkable for his ascents into the upper register; swinging in any range (with Basie, Barnet, Hampton, Ellington).

KING, Teddi. SINGER. B. Boston, Mass., 1929. After her work with George Shearing (1952-53), much of jazz quality has been expected from this singer.

KIRBY, John. BASS. B. Baltimore, Md. 1908; d. Hollywood, Calif., 1952. After important performances with Fletcher Henderson and Chick Webb through much of the thirties, Kirby founded a small band very well known on records and radio for the breadth of its arrangements and the solos of Charlie Shavers, Russell Procope, Buster Bailey, Billy Kyle, O'Neil Spencer (drums), and Kirby.

KIRK, Andy. LEADER. B. Newport, Ky., 1898. Founder and leader of the "Twelve Clouds of Joy" (1929-48). Most famous Clouds: Mary Lou Williams, Dick Wilson, Don Byas, Floyd Smith, Howard McGhee.

KLEIN, Manny. TRUMPET. B. New York, N.Y., 1908. A soloist of distinction with Red Nichols and various studio and recording bands in the years up to and including the first of swing.

KOLLER, Hans. TENOR SAXOPHONE. B. Vienna, Austria, 1921. An impressive modernist, leader of the quartet in which Jutta Hipp achieved her fame in Germany and (through records) elsewhere.

KONITZ, Lee. ALTO SAXOPHONE. B. Chicago, Ill., 1927. Student and colleague of Lennie Tristano, well endowed with melodic resourcefulness, a distinctive tone, and a subtle sense of time, all of which fit well not only with Lennie but with a variety of other, younger, modernists. Among his important appearances: with Miles Davis's Capitol band (1948-50), with Stan Kenton (1952-53), with his own bands (since 1954).

KOTICK, Teddy. BASS. B. Haverhill, Mass., 1928. A ubiquitous rhythm musician among the post-World War II modernists.

KRAL, Roy. PIANO, SINGER, ARRANGER. B. Chicago, Ill., 1921. With wife Jackie Cain a contributor of vocal lines of sprightliness and humor to the Charlie Ventura group (1948-49, 1953) and his own outfits.

KRESS, Carl. GUITAR. B. Newark, N.J., 1907. One of the first to be identified with his instrument as a soloist; with Paul Whiteman, Bix Beiderbecke, Red Nichols, and related recording bands, both as a soloist and in duets with Eddie Lang and Dick McDonough. Later a studio musician.

KRUPA, Gene. DRUMS. B. Chicago, Ill., 1909. An essential part of the Chicago group that formed around McKenzie, Teschemacher, Condon, Goodman, etc. Later (1935-38) the star personality with the Benny Goodman band, well known to millions for his gum chewing and his playing. Off and on since the late thirties a band leader of distinction, concerned to feature such soloists as Roy Eldridge and Charlie Ventura. In recent years Gene has confined his work to small bands and a drum school which he directs along with Cozy Cole.

KYLE, Billy. PIANO. B. Philadelphia, Pa., 1914. In addition to his years with the John Kirby band, Billy has contributed his flowing single-note lines to studio groups, Broadway pit orchestras, and Louis Armstrong.

LADNIER, Tommy. TRUMPET. B. Mandeville, La., 1900; d. New York, N.Y., 1939. A close friend and playing contemporary of Sidney Bechet, with whom he led the New Orleans Feet Warmers in a number of record sessions, as well as ballroom appearances. Well known particularly in New York, where he played off and on from 1925 to 1931.

LAINE, Jack "Papa." DRUMS. B. New Orleans, La., 1873. One of the founding fathers of jazz, leader of a variety of brass bands and small groups, sponsor of dozens of distinguished white jazz musicians in New Orleans from his late teens until shortly after World War I.

LAMARE, Hilton "Nappy." GUITAR. B. New Orleans, La., 1910. Bob

Crosby's fixture as singer, guitarist, personality (1935-42), after some years with Ben Pollack and before a variety of Los Angeles Dixieland employments.

LAMBERT, Dave "Dad." SINGER, ARRANGER. B. Boston, Mass., 1917. After a background as a drummer and a variety of jobs, he developed a bop vocal style with the late Buddy Stewart for Gene Krupa in the mid-forties, later scored for and led a variety of boppish groups of various sizes on and off records.

LAMOND, Don. DRUMS. B. Oklahoma City, Okla., 1920. One of a group of fine modern musicians who developed around Washington, D.C., in the late thirties and early forties, Don took the place of Dave Tough with Woody Herman in 1945, stayed with Woody through 1949, before becoming one of the most reliable and swinging of modern drummers in radio, TV, and record studios in New York.

LANG, Eddie. GUITAR. Philadelphia, Pa., 1904-33. A highly talented melodist who more than any other established the guitar as a solo instrument in his work with the Mound City Blue Blowers, Whiteman, and in a variety of records with Bix, Nichols, and, most famous of all, with Joe Venuti.

LaPORTA, John. CLARINET, ALTO SAXOPHONE, ARRANGER. B. Philadelphia, Pa., 1920. A man of many talents and almost as many playing moods; a modernist of striking individuality who nonetheless has ample respect for most of the jazz traditions and shows it in his writing, and playing with musicians as different from each other as Sonny Russo, Teo Macero, Charlie Mingus, and the Sandole brothers.

LARKINS, Ellis. PIANO. B. Baltimore, Md., 1923. An ample technique and an individual touch characterize Ellis's excellent playing, especially in accompaniment of singers.

LA ROCCA, Dominick James "Nick." CORNET. B. New Orleans, La., 1889. Leader of the Original Dixieland Jazz Band who returned with some small success with a reorganized O.D.J.B. in the late thirties.

LAWRENCE, Elliott. PIANO, LEADER. B. Philadelphia, Pa., 1925. Notable for his sponsorship of such arrangers as Gerry Mulligan and Tiny Kahn and many modern jazz soloists.

LAWSON, Yank. TRUMPET. B. Trenton, Mo., 1911. A vigorous Dixielander with Bob Crosby, Tommy Dorsey, and various recording and radio groups.

LEDBETTER, Huddie "Lead Belly." GUITAR, SINGER. B. Mooringsport, La., 1885; d. New York, N.Y., 1949. Much admired as a folk singer with a captivating personal story (he was twice jailed for murder completed and murder attempted, and his pardon in 1934 by the Governor of Louisiana after singing for him made front pages all over the country). No one particular jazz quality, but with a beat of sorts and a repertory of some interest.

LEE, Julia. SINGER. B. Kansas City, Mo., 1902. One of the best of the blues singers to continue into the modern era.

LEE, Peggy. SINGER. B. Jamestown, N.D., 1920. With Benny Goodman (1941-43); afterward a very successful pop singer capable of a jazz-crafted line and beat.

LEVEY, Stan. DRUMS. B. Philadelphia, Pa., 1925. A Fifty-second Street fixture with bands of all sorts from the bop era until he left to join big bands—most important of them Stan Kenton (1952-54). Most recently a West Coaster and as always a swinging modernist.

LEVY, Louis. PIANO. B. Chicago, Ill., 1928. A skillful post-bop keyboard artist, much experienced with bands such as Georgie Auld, Woody Herman, and various small groups.

LEWIS, George. CLARINET. B. New Orleans, La., 1900. Much admired by those who find the epitome of jazz trumpet in the playing of Bunk Johnson and of jazz piano in the performances of Jelly Roll Morton. Among such, much in demand after the early forties, when the late Gene Williams brought him back into jazz.

LEWIS, John. PIANO, ARRANGER. B. La Grange, Ill., 1920. Well-educated musician with a sharply individual gift as arranger and composer, displayed in large-scale works for Dizzy Gillespie's big band in the late forties and a variety of pieces, classical in structure but never far from jazz in spirit and beat, conceived for the Modern Jazz Quartet, whose musical leader Lewis is.

LEWIS, Meade Lux. PIANO. B. Louisville, Ky., 1905. Another of the early jazz musicians rescued from retirement (by John Hammond) to play countless boogie-woogie solos in clubs and on records during the swing years.

LINN, Ray. TRUMPET. B. Chicago, Ill., 1920. For some years bop's ambassador to the West Coast.

LOMBARDI, Clyde. BASS. B. Bronx, N.Y., 1922. Reliable, swinging performer with all sorts of groups, the modern predominating.

LOWE, Mundell. GUITAR. B. Laurel, Miss., 1922. A Dixieland background in New Orleans led to engagements with Ray McKinley and various small bands in New York. Most recently a studio musician, thoroughly modern in taste and equipment.

LUNCEFORD, Jimmie. LEADER. B. Fulton, Mo., 1902; d. Seaside, Ore., 1947. After mechanical beginnings (1927-34) the Lunceford band became one of the great powerhouse organizations of jazz (incubator of a heavy two-beat style much imitated by other organizations). Sy Oliver was the most important of the band's arrangers at its peak in the late thirties. Lunceford was himself never more than a baton-wielding leader for the band, though he had had a broad musical education at several colleges.

MACERO, Teo. TENOR SAXOPHONE, ARRANGER. B. Glens Falls, N.Y., 1925. Teo emerged from Juilliard with an A.B., an M.A., classical and dance-band experience, and a remarkable ability to combine twelve-tone concepts and jazz procedures in a music which has stayed closer to the second discipline than to the first. He also has had a distinguished career as a composer in a more classical tradition.

MANDEL, Johnny. TROMBONE, BASS TRUMPET, ARRANGER. B. New York, N.Y., 1925. George Handy's most important scoring colleague for the Boyd Raeburn band in the mid-forties; later a close associate of Chubby Jackson and a contributor of scores of various jazz qualities for large and small bands (e.g., Elliott Lawrence, Basie, Chet Baker).

MANN, Herbie. FLUTE. B. Brooklyn, N.Y., 1930. Contributor of tone, taste, and swinging lines to Mat Mathews' quintet (1953-54) and his own groups, and perhaps more responsible than any other single musician for the establishment of the flute in modern jazz.

MANNE, Shelly. DRUMS. B. New York, N.Y., 1920. Fine technician, a swinging musician, who emerged from a big-band background in 1952 to lead important experimental sessions on and off records, up and down southern California.

MANONE, Joseph "Wingy." TRUMPET, SINGER. B. New Orleans, La., 1904. Wingy is so named because his right arm was amputated as a child after a trolley accident. He is a singer, in the Armstrong groove, of considerable wit and style, and capable of at least the necessary beat in his trumpet solos. For years he has been established on the West Coast.

MARABLE, Fate. PIANO. B. Paducah, Ky., 1890; d. St. Louis, Mo., 1947. Most famous of the river-boat leaders. Among his sidemen: Louis Armstrong, Red Allen, the Dodds brothers, Jimmy Blanton.

MARES, Paul. TRUMPET. B. New Orleans, La., 1900; d. Chicago, Ill., 1949. Leader of the New Orleans Rhythm Kings.

MARIANO, Charlie. ALTO SAXOPHONE. B. Boston, Mass., 1923. An articulate modernist with various groups, including Stan Kenton (1953-54).

MARKOWITZ, Irvin "Marky." TRUMPET. B. Washington, D.C., 1923. Another of the Washington group; an imaginative, driving modern.

MARMAROSA, Michael "Dodo." PIANO. B. Pittsburgh, Pa., 1925. An unusually fluent pianist, one of the very best of the early modernists; most recently in retirement because of illness.

MARSALA, Joe. CLARINET. B. Chicago, Ill., 1907. One of the more versatile Dixieland-*cum*-swing musicians, one of the first sponsors of mixed bands.

MARSH, Warne. TENOR SAXOPHONE. B. Los Angeles, Calif., 1927. An elegant sound and melodic resources never fully tapped characterize the playing of this student of Lennie Tristano, close associate of his teacher and of Lee Konitz.

MARSHALL, Kaiser. DRUMS. B. Savannah, Ga., 1902; d. New York, N.Y., 1948. A driving rhythm man with a variety of bands, most important of them Fletcher Henderson (1922-29).

MARSHALL, Wendell. BASS. B. St. Louis, Mo., 1920. Introduced to his instrument by his cousin, Jimmy Blanton, whose position with Ellington he occupied some half-dozen years after Blanton's death (1948-55).

MATHEWS, Mat. ACCORDION. B. The Hague, Netherlands, 1924. Mat turned to music as an escape from forced labor for the Nazis; he became a jazz accordionist under the influence of Joe Mooney, and a thoroughly modern musician on an instrument he designed himself after his arrival in the United States in 1952. The first to make the accordion entirely commendable in jazz.

MATLOCK, Matty. CLARINET. B. Paducah, Ky., 1909. Benny Goodman's replacement with Ben Pollack (1929-34); then Bob Crosby's solo clarinetist.

MATTHEWS, Dave. TENOR SAXOPHONE, ALTO SAXOPHONE, ARRANGER. B. McAllister, Okla., 1911. Famous for his borrowings from Ellington and his rich employment of that style in his arrangements for, among others, Harry James, Hal McIntyre, Woody Herman.

MAXTED, Billy. PIANO. B. Racine, Wis., 1917. A big-band background led Billy to Nick's, where he has remained most of the time since 1949.

MAY, Billy. TRUMPET, ARRANGER. B. Pittsburgh, Pa., 1916. Billy achieved his first reputation as a soloist and arranger for Charlie Barnet (1938-39). His own band in the early fifties featured a unison saxophone section sound which, for all its monotony, did have a jazz feeling.

McCALL, Mary Ann. SINGER. B. Philadelphia, Pa., 1919. For a while in the late forties, with Woody Herman and others, a jazz singer of inspiration, originality, and wit.

McEACHERN, Murray. TROMBONE, ALTO SAXOPHONE. B. Toronto, Ontario, 1915. One of the most versatile of jazz musicians, who has spent most of his musical life in non-jazz surroundings, with the exception of a couple of years with Benny Goodman (1936-38) and various West Coast small bands.

McGARITY, Lou. TROMBONE. B. Athens, Ga., 1917. Swinging Dixielander with Benny Goodman (1940-42, 1946-47).

McGHEE, Howard. TRUMPET. B. Tulsa, Okla., 1918. A bopper of style, beat, and tone, especially in the middle register.

McINTYRE, Hal. ALTO SAXOPHONE. B. Cromwell, Conn., 1914. Glenn Miller's effective lead man, himself a leader of various bands since 1941, the first few of which were notable for their Ellington-influenced library.

McKENZIE, William "Red." SINGER. B. St. Louis, Mo., 1907; d. New York, N.Y., 1948. Leader of the Mound City Blue Blowers, singer, kazoo player, sponsor of many fine jazz musicians in Chicago and on Fifty-second Street in New York. Influential in the development of long-lined, carefully accented jazz singing.

McKIBBON, Al. BASS. B. Chicago, Ill., 1919. A swinger with a tone, closely associated with bop; since 1951 with George Shearing.

McKINLEY, Ray. DRUMS, SINGER. B. Fort Worth, Texas, 1910. Personality with the Dorsey brothers, Jimmy Dorsey, his own band with Will Bradley and alone, Glenn Miller's Air Force outfit, and most recently, leader of another organization arranged around the Miller library.

McKINNEY, William. LEADER. B. Ohio, 1895. Founder and leader of the famous Cotton Pickers, the Detroit band for which Don Redman labored with such distinction, which at one time or another employed musicians of the quality of Benny Carter, Rex Stewart, Joe Smith, etc. The band was a vital part of jazz for well over a decade in the twenties and thirties, ceasing to record in 1933 after half a dozen years of distinguished dates.

McKUSICK, Hal. ALTO SAXOPHONE, CLARINET. B. Medford, Mass., 1924. Settled on the West Coast in the forties, and brought an impressive tone and an able modern style to the Boyd Raeburn band and Claude Thornhill; returned east in 1951 to work with Elliott Lawrence and various small bands.

McPARTLAND, Jimmy. TRUMPET. B. Chicago, Ill., 1907. One of the Austin High gang, who from the mid-thirties led his own little groups, he came back to the United States, after World War II Army experiences, with a new wife (Marian) and a style flexible enough to be at ease with musicians as up-to-date as his wife and as close to Dixieland as those he has used in recordings of tunes associated with Bix Beiderbecke, whose place he took with the Wolverines in the 1920s and whose playing has always much influenced his.

McPARTLAND, Marian. PIANO. B. Windsor, England, 1920. After classical beginnings on the violin, Marian developed a piano style to go with various show-business requirements and considerable fluency as a jazz pianist in the forties. She has been an attractive, much admired part of jazz in the United States since 1946.

McRAE, Carmen. SINGER. B. New York, N.Y., 1922. Of considerable interest to jazz musicians for her work with small bands in the late forties, to larger audiences since the early fifties for her warmth of tone and ability to project a simple, modern melodic line.

McSHANN, Jay. PIANO. B. Muskogee, Okla., 1909. A leader of the jumping Kansas City band which featured Charlie Parker most of the time from 1937 to 1941, but achieved its greatest success with audiences as a result of the blues singing of Walter Brown and the ballads of Al Hibbler.

MEHEGEN, Johnny. PIANO. B. Hartford, Conn., 1920. An articulate teacher (at Juilliard and privately) who can demonstrate his ideas verbally or at the keyboard, as needed.

MELLE, Gil. TENOR SAXOPHONE. B. Riverside, Calif., 1931. Gil's fresh ideas have been heard in several records made in New York in the early fifties, the result of sessions devoted to his writing, playing, and leading.

METTOME, Doug. TRUMPET. B. Salt Lake City, Utah, 1925. One of the first, in the late forties, to absorb bop influences and make them fit effectively in the Herbie Fields, Benny Goodman, Woody Herman, and Tommy Dorsey bands.

MEZZROW, Milt "Mezz." CLARINET. B. Chicago, Ill., 1899. According to Hugues Panassié, "Not only one of the great clarinets but one of the great white jazz musicians, he has assimilated the traditional style so perfectly that when he plays you think you are listening to a clarinet from New Orleans." It is difficult to find other critics or musicians who will place themselves on record as in any way admiring his playing on the clarinet or saxophone. He did, however, lead some effective record sessions in the early thirties and has been an effective pleader for the Negro people in articles and his book, *Really the Blues*.

MILEY, James "Bubber." TRUMPET. B. Aiken, S.C., 1903; d. 1932. Founder of the plunger trumpet style, with Duke Ellington. A growler of great style with Ellington from 1925 to 1929.

MILLER, Eddie. TENOR SAXOPHONE. B. New Orleans, La., 1911. A particularly persuasive ballad performer with Bob Crosby (1936-42) and on the West Coast afterward.

MILLER, Glenn. TROMBONE, ARRANGER. B. Clarinda, Iowa, 1904; disappeared on a flight from England to France, 1944. Never much of a jazz performer, Glenn did write some swinging scores for Red Nichols, the Dorseys, Ray Noble, and his own bands.

MILLINDER, Lucius "Lucky." LEADER. B. Anniston, Ala., 1900. With the Mills Blue Rhythm Band in the early thirties, which he took over under his own name in 1934. Lucky has long been gifted with the ability to spot and hire able musicians. The earlier editions of his band included most of the John Kirby group, Harry Edison, Red Allen, and J. C. Higginbotham. Among the modernists who played with him were the late Freddie Webster, Dizzy Gillespie, Joe Guy, Lucky Thompson, the late Clyde Hart, and George Duvivier.

MILLS BROTHERS, SINGERS. B. Ohio: Albert (1912), Harry (1913), Donald (1915). For twenty years, starting in 1946, John Mills, Sr. (B. Bellefonte, Pa., 1889), father of the brothers, acted as anchor man following the death of his son, John, Jr. The group has always been distinguished for precise intonation, a beat, the ability to fit in with all sorts of styles, in and out of jazz. For no other vocal group can as much be said.

MINCE, Johnny. CLARINET. B. Chicago Heights, Ill., 1912. Particularly well known during the swing years as a jazz soloist with Ray Noble (1934-35) and Tommy Dorsey (1936-41).

MINGUS, Charlie. BASS, COMPOSER. B. Nogales, Ariz., 1922. Variously educated, formally and informally; variously gifted as a performer and writer of jazz. His West Coast playing experience included big bands (Louis Armstrong and Lionel Hampton) and small (Lee Young, Red Norvo). On the East Coast, since the early fifties, Mingus has made a profound impression as an experimental writer for his own groups and one or two others, for records and concerts and clubs. Little awed by conventional tradition, he has worked hard to develop a style in his playing and his writing which can make as much as possible of the potentialities of his instrument and others. As a soloist he is gifted with technique, a very large tone, and a fine beat.

MITCHELL, Red. BASS. B. New York, N.Y., 1927. A flexible modernist of considerable experience: Chubby Jackson's big band, Woody Herman, the Norvo Trio, the Mulligan Quartet, the Hampton Hawes Trio.

MITCHELL, Whitey. BASS. B. Hackensack, N.J., 1932. Whitey is Red's brother and, like him, at ease among his contemporaries in contemporary styles.

MOLE, Milfred "Miff." TROMBONE. B. Roosevelt, L.I., N.Y., 1898. An able Dixieland sideman and leader with all sorts of groups on and off records in the twenties and thirties—the Memphis Five, the Molers, Red Nichols, etc. Later jobs include brief appearances with Paul Whiteman, Benny Goodman, and a variety of Nicksieland groups.

MONK, Thelonious. PIANO, COMPOSER. B. New York, N.Y., 1920. One of the original boppers of a considerable individuality, particularly effective in the construction of fresh melodic lines of interest to boppers and post-boppers. As a performer something less than facile.

MONTROSE, Jack. TENOR SAXOPHONE, ARRANGER. B. Detroit, Mich., 1928. A well-equipped West Coast musician who works with impressive deliberateness, particularly in constructing his scores, which, while influenced by several contemporary classical styles, continue to preserve a jazz flavor.

MOODY, James. TENOR SAXOPHONE, ALTO SAXOPHONE. B. Savannah, Ga., 1925. Particularly effective in the mid-bop years as a tenor soloist.

MOONEY, Joe. ACCORDION, PIANO, ORGAN, SINGER. B. Jersey City, N.J., 1911. Versatile musician of an impressive delicacy of tone and a corollary gift for understatement, both in his playing and singing.

MOORE, Billy, Jr. PIANO, ARRANGER. B. Parkersburg, W. Va., 1917. Sy Oliver's successor as jazz arranger for Lunceford (1939); for some years the inspired writer of original scores of jazz wit and wisdom.

MOORE, Brew. TENOR SAXOPHONE. B. Indianola, Miss., 1925. One of the best of Lester Young-influenced tenor men who popped up in such number in the bop era. Most recently a San Francisco performer of note.

MOORE, Oscar. GUITAR. B. Austin, Texas, 1916. King Cole Trio guitarist (1937-47), justly famous for his simple, swinging single-string lines.

MORELLO, Joe. DRUMS. B. Springfield, Mass., 1928. A superb small-band performer of restraint and delicacy and beat.

MORTON, Benny. TROMBONE. B. New York, N.Y., 1907. A soloist of vigor and warmth of two eras: featured with Fletcher Henderson and Don Redman in the late twenties and thirties, he was later an important part of swing with Count Basie, Teddy Wilson, and his own groups. Of late a performer with Broadway pit bands, and in the studios.

MORTON, Ferdinand "Jelly Roll." PIANO, COMPOSER. B. Gulfport, La., 1885; d. Los Angeles, Calif., 1941. Controversial figure, a musician who did as well in his reminiscences (in book form and on records) as in his performances. For some he is a giant of New Orleans jazz; for others there is little in his simple formulations at the keyboard or on paper of particular musical interest, except a few figures which other jazz musicians improved upon in their arrangements or solos. There is no doubt, however, that he contributed to jazz some of its best-known early-session figurations, those that go by the names of "King Porter Stomp," "Milenburg Joys," "Wild Man Blues," "Shoe Shiner's Drag," etc.

MOST, Sam. FLUTE, CLARINET. B. Atlantic City, N.J., 1930. Long with Herbie Mann, Sam has done much to establish the flute in modern jazz. Like his brother, Abe, he is also a fluent clarinetist.

MOTEN, Bennie. PIANO. Kansas City, Mo., 1894-1935. Important as leader of the K.C. band which evolved, after Bennie's death, into the Count Basie organization.

MULLIGAN, Gerry. BARITONE SAXOPHONE, ARRANGER. B. New York, N.Y., 1927. After auspicious beginnings as an arranger in New York and Philadelphia in the late forties, Gerry developed the quartet without a piano (trumpet, baritone, bass, drums) which has been indelibly associated with his name ever since. He has sometimes substituted the valve trombone for the trumpet and has worked since 1955 with a sextet, but it is the original group, featuring Chet Baker and himself, with Chico Hamilton on drums, which made indisputable Gerry's skill as a maker of soft sounds and constructor of deft melodies and counter-melodies.

MUNDY, James. ARRANGER. B. Cincinnati, Ohio, 1907. One of the best writers of driving instrumentals for Benny Goodman, Count Basie, and others in the swing era.

MURPHY, Lyle "Spud." ARRANGER. B. Salt Lake City, Utah, 1908. Scripter of swing pieces in the swing epoch who has turned successfully to a kind of twelve-tone method of his own devising, which he has improved in arranging, composing, and teaching on the West Coast since the mid-fifties.

MURPHY, Turk. TROMBONE, ARRANGER. B. Palermo, Calif., 1915. One of the leaders of the San Francisco revival of New Orleans jazz since the early forties. Originally with the Lu Watters band; since 1947 leader of his own group, which after the mid-fifties, in several recordings, had achieved something like nationwide success.

MUSSO, Vido. TENOR SAXOPHONE. B. Carrini, Sicily, 1913. Big-toned, simple-styled tenor saxophonist in the Hawkins fashion, of particular importance in the late thirties and forties with (among others) Benny Goodman, Gene Krupa, Woody Herman, Stan Kenton.

NANCE, Ray. TRUMPET, VIOLIN. B. Chicago, Ill., 1913. A clever, all-around performer known as "Floor Show" among the Ellington musicians after 1940. Earlier an effective performer with Earl Hines and Horace Henderson, and around Chicago night clubs.

NANTON, Joseph "Tricky Sam." TROMBONE. B. New York, N.Y., 1904; d. San Francisco, Calif., 1948. Duke's growler (1926-48), equally effective in solos of a touching or humorous nature.

NAPOLEON, Phil. TRUMPET. B. Boston, Mass., 1901. Of major importance in jazz as leader of the original Memphis Five; later (early fifties), after commercial career, once again well known as a Dixielander.

NAVARRO, Theodore "Fats." TRUMPET. B. Key West, Fla., 1923; d. New York, N.Y., 1950. Bop's most elegant performer, Fats developed his fluent technique and beautiful tone with the bands of Andy Kirk, Billy Eckstine, Lionel Hampton, Coleman Hawkins, and various small bop groups at Minton's and downtown in New York in the late forties.

NERO, PAUL. VIOLIN. B. Hamburg, Germany, 1917. A superbly educated (Curtis Institute) musician who has since the late thirties dedicated virtuoso talents to playing and writing jazz directed at making his violin a logical swinging part of jazz.

NEWBORN, Phineas, Jr. PIANO. B. Whiteville, Tenn., 1931. After desultory beginnings, Phineas found his rainbow in modern jazz in New York in 1956. He is a bravura performer of some real experimental interest, with perhaps too much determination to be showy.

NEWMAN, Joe. TRUMPET. B. New Orleans, La., 1922. An effective, punchy performer with Lionel Hampton (1941-42) and Count Basie (1943-46 and from 1952 on).

NEWTON, Frankie. TRUMPET. B. Emory, Va., 1906; d. New York, N.Y., 1954. Variously effective swing musician in the thirties and early forties.

NICHOLAS, Albert. CLARINET. B. New Orleans, La., 1900. An effective second-generation New Orleans musician who achieved a reputation in later years with Luis Russell (off and on from 1928 to 1939). Most recently a part of the French jazz scene.

NICHOLS, Ernest Loring "Red." CORNET. B. Ogden, Utah, 1905. Enormously successful record-session leader in the late twenties; later a big-band leader of some prominence and then, in more recent years, a Los Angeles Dixieland performer. Overshadowed by Bix but by no means as poor a representative of that school of cornet playing as some of his critics have suggested.

NIEHAUS, Lennie. ALTO SAXOPHONE. B. St. Louis, Mo., 1929. Well educated on the West Coast and a most articulate and musicianly representative of his school and of his instrument with small bands and with Stan Kenton off and on from 1952.

NOBLE, Ray. LEADER. B. Brighton, England, 1907. Of brief significance to jazz in the United States in 1934 and 1935, when he hired musicians of the caliber of Bud Freeman, Will Bradley, Glenn Miller, and Claude Thornhill.

NOONE, Jimmie. CLARINET. B. New Orleans, La., 1895; d. Los Angeles, Calif., 1944. Biggest-toned and perhaps most skillful of all New Orleans clarinetists, who reached his peak, properly enough, at the Apex Club in Chicago in the late twenties with Earl Hines featured as his small band's pianist. Noone influenced, among others, such clarinetists as Benny Goodman and Jimmy Dorsey.

NORVO, Red. VIBRAPHONE, XYLOPHONE. B. Beardstown, Ill., 1908. After several bands of his own and a brief career with Paul Whiteman, he and Mildred Bailey, who was then his wife, founded first a small band (1934), then a medium-sized outfit (1936) which was one of the most tasteful and—musically, at least—one of the most successful of swing bands. In the forties he led a series of small groups, switched to vibes (1943), played with Benny Goodman and Woody Herman and founded a trio (1949) with which he has been working ever since out of California. Always a performer of taste and skill, Norvo has always surrounded himself with musicians of similar qualities; in the trio, for example, his guitarists have been Tal Farlow and Jimmy Raney, his bass players Charlie Mingus and Red Mitchell.

O'BRIEN, Floyd. TROMBONE. B. Chicago, Ill., 1904. A significant barrelhouse musician in the twenties in Chicago and later with bands such as those of Gene Krupa, Bob Crosby, Jack Teagarden. Most recently a gigging Dixielander and teacher in Chicago.

O'DAY, Anita. SINGER. B. Chicago, Ill., 1919. An extraordinary gift for turning a hoarse voice and an odd sense of phrasing into swinging lines made Anita an immediate success with Gene Krupa in 1941 and later with Stan Kenton (1944-45) and in all sorts of appearances as a single.

OLIVER, Joseph "King." CORNET. B. New Orleans, La., 1885; d. Savannah, Ga., 1938. One of the most important of the alumni of New Orleans brass bands, teacher and first important leader of

Louis Armstrong (who joined him in Chicago in 1922), and perhaps most important of all bandsmen in promoting the dispersal of jazz from New Orleans to points north, east, and west. After his failure to accept the Cotton Club date in December 1927 for which Duke Ellington filled in, Oliver gradually ceased to play an important role in jazz and was an obscure man by the time of his death.

OLIVER, Sy. TRUMPET, ARRANGER. B. Battle Creek, Mich., 1910. A gifted musician, able ballad singer, capable sideman, and creator of the heavy two-beat style associated with Lunceford (1933-39), Tommy Dorsey (for whom he wrote after 1939), and all sorts of recording bands which he led for several New York companies in the forties and fifties.

ORY, Edward "Kid." TROMBONE. B. La Place, La., 1886. A versatile musician who played trumpet in New Orleans before switching to the slide horn in California in the twenties, which instrument he played with King Oliver (1925-27) and as a vital part of Louis Armstrong's recording Hot Five. After a decade of retirement he returned to jazz in 1940, one of the oldtimers most respected by followers of New Orleans jazz for his gutbucket style.

PAGE, Oran "Hot Lips." TRUMPET, SINGER. B. Dallas, Texas, 1908; d. New York, N.Y., 1954. A swinging, colorful part of Kansas City jazz from 1927 to 1936, when he left the Count Basie band to develop a career as a small-band musician (with a brief appearance in 1941 with Artie Shaw). A Dixieland trumpeter, gravel-throated singer.

PAGE, Walter. BASS. B. Gallatin, Mo., 1900. Leader of a Kansas City band of some importance in the late twenties, then with Bennie Moten (1931) and Count Basie (off and on from 1935-38), with whom he achieved fame as part of the Basie-Greene-Jones-Page rhythm section.

PARKER, Charlie "Yard Bird," "Bird." ALTO SAXOPHONE. B. Kansas City, Mo., 1920; d. New York, N.Y., 1955. Musicians who heard Bird with Jay McShann (at various times from 1937-41) were quite impressed by the fluent melodic lines he developed, his beat, his unusual sound. Those who heard him in New York, with Earl Hines, with Billy Eckstine, and with his own little bands, after 1942, were bowled over by these same qualities developed to such a point that when a breakdown sent him to a state hospital in California in 1946, it was accounted a calamity for jazz. From 1947 until his death he contributed figures, playing procedures, a sense of time, and a continuity to modern jazz which no one on any instrument has quite matched, but which scores of moderns on every instrument have tried to imitate.

PARKER, Leo. BARITONE SAXOPHONE. B. Washington, D.C., 1925. In early appearances in the early bop years, Leo established the suitability of his horn for the new music.

PAUL, Les. GUITAR. B. Waukesha, Wis., 1916. Briefly between careers with Fred Waring and with his wife Mary Ford, Les led a swinging modern trio (1944-46). Always, as millions recognized from records of no particular jazz importance, a musical wit and technically resourceful; once something more than that, an eloquent jazzman.

PAYNE, Cecil. BARITONE SAXOPHONE. B. Brooklyn, N.Y., 1922. A splendid bopper, with Dizzy Gillespie (1946-49), Tadd Dameron, and others.

PEIFFER, Bernard. PIANO. B. Epinard, France, 1922. Superbly trained at the Marseille Conservatory and the École Normale in Paris, an improviser in the great French classical tradition and a jazz musician of swinging warmth as well as breathtaking technique.

PEPPER, Art. ALTO SAXOPHONE. B. Gardena, Calif., 1925. An agile modernist with a strong bop flavor, best known for his work with Stan Kenton (off and on 1943-52).

PERKINS, Bill. TENOR SAXOPHONE. B. San Francisco, Calif., 1924. Much featured, much admired in 1956 and 1957 with Stan Kenton and on his own records. As a stylist he leans toward Lester Young.

PETERSON, Oscar. PIANO. B. Toronto, Ontario, 1925. Well-trained, slick performer of Tatumesque skill and particular persuasiveness in developing, in a florid style, swinging melodic lines.

PETTIFORD, Oscar. BASS, CELLO. B. Okmulgee, Okla., 1922. Generally well trained by a musically gifted family and an immediate success after joining Charlie Barnet in 1943, Oscar was of signal importance as leader and bass player in the formative years of bop. Later his large-toned and superlative technique brought him success with Duke Ellington (1945-48) on bass and as a cellist with a variety of small groups in the early fifties.

PHILLIPS, Joseph "Flip." TENOR SAXOPHONE. B. Brooklyn, N.Y., 1915. A powerhouse performer most impressive musically in ballads of the kind he played so well with Woody Herman from 1944 to 1946.

PICOU, Alphonse. CLARINET. New Orleans, La., 1878-1957. One of the best known of the early clarinetists, particularly for his polka-like "High Society" solo.

PIERCE, Nat. PIANO, ARRANGER. B. Somerville, Mass., 1925. Leader of a local band of distinction in the late forties, then a Woody Herman mainstay in the early fifties. Effective as performer and scripter in the Basie groove.

POLLACK, Ben. DRUMS. B. Chicago, Ill., 1903. A drummer with several Chicago groups in the early twenties, including that version of the New Orleans Rhythm Kings which was known as the Friars Society Orchestra. As a band leader in the late twenties and thirties, the sponsor of Benny Goodman, Jimmy McPartland, Glenn Miller. Later Ben introduced Harry James and Irving Fazola to jazz audiences.

POLO, Danny. CLARINET. B. Clinton, Ind., 1901; d. Chicago, Ill., 1949. A warm, round-toned soloist with Jean Goldkette, various European orchestras in the twenties and thirties, a variety of small bands and Claude Thornhill on his return to the States after 1939.

POTTER, Tommy. BASS. B. Philadelphia, Pa., 1918. An essential part of bop and post-bop jazz in and around New York.

POWELL, Benny. TROMBONE. B. New Orleans, La., 1930. Skillful post-bopper with small bands, Lionel Hampton (1948-51), Count Basie (after 1951).

POWELL, Earl "Bud." PIANO. B. New York, N.Y., 1924. The most fertile imagination among bop pianists is Bud's, coupled with an extraordinary drive, a superb sense of structure, and substantial melodic resources. His imaginative talents sometimes seem to be very close in importance to those of Charlie Parker. Unfortunately, he has long been subject to breakdowns which have removed him from time to time from jazz.

POWELL, Mel. PIANO, ARRANGER. B. New York, N.Y., 1923. A skillful creator of adventurous manuscript for Benny Goodman in the early forties, and again off and on in later years. More recently a teacher of theory at Queens College in New York. As a performer, he is best characterized as an adventurous, astute Dixielander.

POWELL, Seldon. TENOR SAXOPHONE. B. Lawrenceville, Va., 1928. A large sound and facile technique stamp Seldon as one of the few performers who in recent years have added anything new in the way of personality to the playing of his instrument, on which it may be said that he arrived in 1956, on and off records.

POZO, Chano. BONGO AND CONGA DRUMS. B. Matanzas, Cuba, 1920; d. New York, N.Y., 1948. Early eloquent performer of Afro-Cuban rhythmic lines, never quite matched by anybody else who attempted the same exotic instrument.

PREVIN, André. PIANO, ARRANGER. B. Berlin, Germany, 1929. Splendidly trained, widely gifted classical musician who over the years (since 1944) has been trying his expressive hands at jazz, has become more and more a swinging performer and writer of modern jazz.

PROCOPE, Russell. ALTO SAXOPHONE. B. New York, N.Y., 1908. An articulate representative of his instrument with Chick Webb,

Fletcher Henderson, Benny Carter, Teddy Hill, John Kirby (1938-45), and Duke Ellington (since 1945).

QUEBEC, Ike. TENOR SAXOPHONE. B. Newark, N.J., 1918. Ike's barrel-sized sound was well fitted to the Hawkins groove. He has worked easily and well with all sorts of small bands, and with Hawkins himself (from 1944 to 1951).

QUINICHETTE, Paul. TENOR SAXOPHONE. B. Denver, Colo., 1921. An assiduous follower in the path of Lester Young and an able one with small bands especially, and for several years with Count Basie (1951-53).

RAEBURN, Boyd. LEADER. B. Faith, S.D., 1913. A leader of taste during the mid-forties who in his choice of musicians and arrangements has belied his society and Mickey Mouse band background. His most important arrangers were George Handy, Johnny Mandel, and Johnny Richards, his most important musicians the Washington crowd, Don Lamond and Earl Swope, and such other distinguished men who worked for him on and off records as Hal McKusick, Frankie Socolow, Sonny Berman, and Dizzy Gillespie.

RAINEY, Gene. BASS. B. Austin, Texas, 1913. Out of Kansas City by way of Jay McShann's band (1938-44) to Fifty-second Street, bop, and Count Basie (1952-53), Gene has long been impressive for a big, booting tone.

RAINEY, Gertrude "Ma." SINGER. Columbus, Ga., 1886-1939. Bessie Smith's mentor, a swinging, well-organized blues singer who made many impressive recordings of music of this genre.

RANDOLPH, Irving "Mouse." TRUMPET. B. St. Louis, Mo., 1909. A much-experienced musician, from river boats to Fletcher Henderson, Cab Calloway (1935-39), Chick Webb, and a variety of small bands.

RANEY, Jimmy. GUITAR. B. Louisville, Ky., 1927. A brilliantly individual musician who in small bands (Stan Getz, Red Norvo) and large (notably Woody Herman in 1948) has shown himself capable of fresh ideas, a lovely tone, and great continuity.

RAPPOLO, Leon. CLARINET. B. Lutheran, La., 1902; d. Jackson, La., 1943. Auspicious beginnings with the New Orleans Rhythm Kings in the early twenties came to a tragic end when mental illness afflicted Rappolo. A man of large melodic gifts and an original, swinging style.

REARDON, Casper. HARP. B. Little Falls, N.Y., 1907; d. New York, N.Y., 1941. First to show the jazz potentialities of his instrument as a single in small supper clubs and on records and one or two dates with Jack Teagarden in the mid-thirties.

REDMAN, Don. ALTO SAXOPHONE, ARRANGER. B. Piedmont, W. Va., 1900. A conservatory-trained musician of great breadth, both of taste and equipment, Don made his jazz debut with the Fletcher Henderson band in 1923, directed McKinney's Cotton Pickers from 1929 to 1931, and spent the rest of the thirties leading a fine orchestra, a successful one with an unusual library, having more than its share of fresh scores contributed chiefly by its leader. Don's contribution to records, his own and others' (Louis Armstrong, Chocolate Dandies, etc.), is particularly impressive on the alto, on which his fluency and resourceful melodic development remind one of Benny Carter, but he also was capable of effective soprano saxophone and singing contributions. In recent years he has been associated with Pearl Bailey as arranger and leader.

REINHARDT, Django. GUITAR. B. Liverchies, Belgium, 1910; d. Fontainebleau, France, 1953. The gypsy background and freak style Django developed to surmount the difficulties caused by the loss of two fingers of his left hand made him an irresistible personality in European jazz in the thirties and forties. His beat, his attractive tone, his ability to grow with the times, add to his appeal as one listens to records made over the years with the Quintet of The Hot Club of France and other groups in the last years of his life.

RICH, Buddy. DRUMS. B. Brooklyn, N.Y., 1917. A technician of great skill with the bands of Bunny Berigan, Artie Shaw, Tommy Dorsey, and his own group, and a showman of similar skill

(Buddy is capable of a very attractive cozening singing performance of large jazz parts).

RICHARDS, Johnny. ARRANGER. B. Schenectady, N.Y., 1911. An effective translator of classical idiom into jazz scores for Boyd Raeburn, Stan Kenton, Dizzy Gillespie (and strings in 1950), Sarah Vaughan, and various ensembles he has himself led.

ROACH, Max. DRUMS. B. Brooklyn, N.Y., 1925. A bopper from his beginnings with Charlie Parker and others at the Uptown House, Minton's, and on the Street in the early forties, Max has, more than any other drummer in our time, turned his instrument from the minor patrolman's function of walking the beat to the artist's role of establishing lines of his own. Most felicitous examples of his work can be found on records with Bird and Dizzy, with Clifford Brown (with whom he toured from 1954 to 1956), and with Bud Powell, whose imagination he has matched marvelously well.

ROCHE, Betty. SINGER. B. Wilmington, Del., 1920. An intriguingly inventive singer, with Duke Ellington (1943-44, 1952-53).

RODNEY, Red. TRUMPET. B. Philadelphia, Pa., 1927. One of those who was able effectively to assimilate bop influences into an individual style in the middle and late forties, especially in work with small bands.

ROGERS, Milton "Shorty." TRUMPET, ARRANGER. B. Great Barrington, Mass., 1924. Educated formally in classical traditions, informally in Red Norvo (1942-43), Woody Herman (off and on from 1945 to 1949), and West Coast (from 1953 on) playing and thinking procedures. Shorty is a hard-working, much-employed arranger who has been able to translate modern jazz ideas and atmospheres effectively into studio scores as well as large- and small-band arrangements. As a trumpeter he is an effective post-bopper, small of tone, precise of figure.

ROLLINI, Adrian. VIBRAPHONE, BASS SAXOPHONE. B. New York, N.Y., 1904; d. Homestead, Fla., 1956. An important part of jazz in the twenties and thirties, moving from his deep-voiced sax into the vibes, from which latter instrument he led a considerable variety of date records of distinction in the early years of swing.

ROLLINS, Sonny. TENOR SAXOPHONE. B. New York, N.Y., 1929. A bopper who expanded from the merely imitative to the considerably individual as his career moved from alto to tenor and across the decade from the mid-forties to the mid-fifties.

ROSOLINO, Frank. TROMBONE. B. Detroit, Mich., 1926. A bumptious post-bopper who has enlivened several bands, notably those of Gene Krupa (1948-49) and Stan Kenton (1953-54).

ROYAL, Ernie. TRUMPET. B. Los Angeles, Calif., 1921. A musician much admired by other musicians for his fluency in many styles and his precise technique in performances with West Coast bands in the forties, with Count Basie (1946), Woody Herman (1947), Duke Ellington (1950), Stan Kenton (1953), and a variety of small bands.

RUGOLO, Pete. PIANO, ARRANGER. B. San Piero, Patti, Sicily, 1915. A California musician who brought force and conviction to Kenton jazz from 1945 to 1949 and has been able from time to time since at least to suggest his own jazz skills in arrangements for many singers and a short-lived but thoroughly enjoyable big band of his own in late 1954.

RUSHING, Jimmy. SINGER. B. Oklahoma City, Okla., 1903. A Kansas City figure of size (he is the original figure described as "Mr. Five by Five") from the late twenties to 1936, when he left K.C. with the Basie band, whose identifying blues voice he was until 1950.

RUSHTON, Joe. BASS SAXOPHONE. B. Evanston, Ill., 1907. One of the very few to turn his booming instrument into a musically acceptable voice in stints with big bands (Ted Weems, Benny Goodman, Horace Heidt) and small, the latter chiefly of the Dixieland variety. Versatile, witty, on and off his horn.

RUSSELL, Charles Ellsworth "Pee Wee." CLARINET. B. St. Louis, Mo., 1906. One of the famous Chicago gang of the 1920s, a Nicksieland musician of distinction, gifted with a charming eccentricity of tone.

RUSSELL, Curley. BASS. B. New York, N.Y., 1920. One of bop's hardest and most reliable workers. Particularly impressive in his close following of Bud Powell.

RUSSELL, George. ARRANGER. B. Cincinnati, Ohio, 1923. Writer of large-scale bop pieces with Afro-Cuban influences for Dizzy Gillespie; of late concerned to develop a system of his own based on one of the ancient modes, the Lydian.

RUSSELL, Luis, PIANO. B. Bocas del Toro, Panama, 1902. As a reader of this section of the book will have recognized by now, Russell was a vital figure in the twenties, thirties, and forties as leader of a band through which passed some of the best jazz musicians of the several eras involved, and as a collaborator with many musicians, most importantly with Louis Armstrong.

RUSSO, Bill. TROMBONE, ARRANGER. B. Chicago, Ill., 1928. An effective experimental writer for concertizing Chicago groups and for Stan Kenton (since 1950).

RUSSO, Sonny. TROMBONE. B. Brooklyn, N.Y., 1929. A big-band performer who, in the fifties, demonstrated a kind of modern barrelhouse style of wit and imagination.

SACHS, Aaron. CLARINET, TENOR SAXOPHONE. B. Bronx, N.Y., 1923. An articulate representative of semi-modern and modern styles on both his instruments, with Red Norvo, Benny Goodman, Earl Hines, and others in the forties and fifties.

SAFRANSKI, Ed. BASS. B. Pittsburgh, Pa., 1918. Much admired for tone, taste, and technique, especially in his Hal McIntyre (1941-45) and Stan Kenton (1945-48) days.

SALVADOR, Sal. GUITAR. B. Monson, Mass., 1925. A modernist who inflects ballad lines with particular persuasiveness. His small bands, formed after leaving Stan Kenton (1952-53), have featured an effective pairing of Sal and pianist Eddie Costa.

SAMPSON, Edgar. ARRANGER. B. New York, N.Y., 1907. Performer on alto and tenor at various times, Sampson is particularly important for the tunes he created for the Chick Webb band and others who inevitably picked up his swinging figures, such tunes as "Blue Lou," "Stompin' at the Savoy," "Don't Be That Way," "Lullaby in Rhythm."

SAUTER, Eddie. ARRANGER. B. Brooklyn, N.Y., 1914. Writer of freshness and fluency for Red Norvo (1935-39), Benny Goodman (through most of the forties), and his own band (led together with Bill Finegan since 1952). Eddie's style has matched an intriguing combination of traditional jazz procedures and thoroughly up-to-date modern classical idiom.

SCHILDKRAUT, Dave. ALTO SAXOPHONE. B. New York, N.Y., 1925. One of the most fluent of modern altoists, who has brought the Parker style to an effective place in the large band (notably with Stan Kenton in 1953).

SCHOEBEL, Elmer. PIANO. B. East St. Louis, Ill., 1896. A significant performer and writer for such early Dixie groups as the New Orleans Rhythm Kings and several of its successors, and later a successful song writer ("Farewell Blues," "Bugle Call Rag," "Nobody's Sweetheart," etc.) and arranger.

SCHULLER, Gunther. FRENCH HORN, COMPOSER. B. Jackson Heights, N.Y., 1925. A musician who works as a performer and composer in the classical world but turns with remarkable ease to jazz and has written effectively for several small bands and may be expected to work more and more into jazz in future. If he must be tied to a school, his associations may be said to be chiefly twelve-tone.

SCOTT, Bobby. PIANO. B. Bronx, N.Y., 1937. One of the more articulate young keyboard performers of modern persuasion.

SCOTT, Bud. BANJO, GUITAR. B. New Orleans, La., 1890; d. Los Angeles, Calif., 1949. A musician of some importance with the King Oliver band in the twenties, other Chicago outfits, and, in the last half-dozen years of his life, with Kid Ory and Louis Armstrong.

SCOTT, Raymond. LEADER. B. Brooklyn, N.Y., 1910. A facile scripter, particularly important to jazz for his sponsorship, in radio in the late thirties and early forties, first of swing and then of fairly modern jazz bands.

SCOTT, Tony. CLARINET. B. Morristown, N.J., 1921. Broadly experienced, a performer of catholic tastes and round tone who has developed in the fifties into a particularly effective balladier and a modernist of attractively mixed moods, leading small and large bands, especially for recording.

SEARS, Al. TENOR SAXOPHONE. B. Macomb, Ill., 1910. An infectious staccato beat characterizes Sears' work, which with Duke Ellington (off and on from 1943 to 1951) offered an always pleasant counterpoise to the sleek sounds of the other saxes.

SHANK, Bud. ALTO SAXOPHONE, FLUTE. B. Dayton, Ohio, 1926. A musician of ease on several reed instruments and one of the most frequently satisfying performers on the two instruments listed above in West Coast recordings.

SHAVERS, Charlie. TRUMPET. B. New York, N.Y., 1917. A phenomenally skillful technician who emerged from years with the John Kirby band to find himself widely in demand and to yield to the demand in various alliances with Raymond Scott, Tommy Dorsey, Benny Goodman, etc.

SHAW, Artie. CLARINET. B. New York, N.Y., 1910. An experimenter to begin with (his 1935 band featuring a string quartet), an enormously successful leader of a swing band (1937-39), a sometime chief of a conventional mixture of strings and jazz instrumentation (off and on in the forties), and throughout it all much married to ideas as well as to women. Gifted as a performer and endowed with extraordinary intellectual gifts, Artie has never quite developed into the musician that his endowments have suggested he could or would at any time become.

SHEARING, George. PIANO. B. London, England, 1919. Articulate at the keyboard, a fashioner of a fashionable style for piano, vibes, and rhythm, which since 1949 has been a very successful part of jazz and pop music in America (to which he emigrated in 1947).

SHIELDS, Larry. CLARINET. B. New Orleans, La., 1893; d. Hollywood, Calif., 1953. Clarinetist with the Original Dixieland Jazz Band, a humorist of sorts, and gifted with a beat.

SIGNORELLI, Frank. PIANO. B. New York, N.Y., 1901. One of the Original Dixieland Jazz Band and the Original Memphis Five and a close associate of Bix, Venuti, Lang, and Red Nichols.

SILVER, Horace. PIANO. B. Norwalk, Conn., 1928. Influenced by Bud Powell but an individualist of skill in constructing figures of his own devising as well as those of other musicians; one of the most distinguished of the post-boppers.

SIMEON, Omer. CLARINET. B. New Orleans, La., 1902. A Dixielander notable for his adaptability to later styles in jazz (e.g., Earl Hines, Jimmie Lunceford).

SIMS, Zoot. TENOR SAXOPHONE. B. Inglewood, Calif., 1925. One of Woody Herman's Four Brothers (1947-49) and one of the most booting of the Lester Young-inspired tenor men.

SINATRA, Frank. SINGER. B. Hoboken, N.J., 1915. One of the most effective assimilations of jazz into popular singing was made by Frank, especially in the years after his band associations (Harry James, Tommy Dorsey), in the late forties and fifties.

SINGLETON, Zutty. DRUMMER. B. Bunkie, La., 1898. More than a Dixieland drummer of skill, a personality of charm in several kinds of jazz, from New Orleans to West Coast swing, in the late thirties and forties.

SMITH, Bessie. SINGER. B. Chattanooga, Tenn., ca. 1895; d. Clarksdale, Miss., 1937. In everything—her voice, her bearing, her beat, her ability to work with the finest jazz musicians of her day —thoroughly entitled to the description the "Empress of the Blues." Her career had ups and downs, but never in the memory of any of those who heard her, and on none of the records she made in the mid-twenties, did she fall below the highest level of blues singing. Some of her recording associates: Louis Armstrong,

Fletcher Henderson, Joe Smith, Jack Teagarden. Her tragic death occurred when she was turned away from a segregated hospital after an automobile crash: she died from loss of blood while being sped to one that admitted Negroes.

SMITH, Clarence "Pinetop." PIANO. B. Troy, Ala., 1904; d. Chicago, Ill., 1929. A legendary blues singer whose presence on records is solid enough and who left behind some of the most swinging examples of his boogie-woogie style and figures he constructed to display it.

SMITH, Hezekiah Leroy Gordon "Stuff." VIOLIN. B. Portsmouth, Ohio, 1909. An altogether delightful musician who, in the late thirties and all through the forties, led groups distinguished for all-around jazz skill which created excellent settings for his unconventional, thoroughly swinging fiddling.

SMITH, Jabbo. TRUMPET, SINGER. B. Claxton, Ga., 1908. A witty performer, especially with Claude Hopkins in the mid-thirties.

SMITH, Jimmy. ORGAN. B. Morristown, Pa., 1925. Of all those who have turned to the instrument driven by electrons, Jimmy has made most effective use of the amplified sounds created on the manuals and the pedals and with the stops. He is, as his 1956 records closely demonstrate, a performer of considerable depth and an infectious beat.

SMITH, Joe. TRUMPET. B. Ripley, Ohio, 1902; d. New York, N.Y., 1937. Gifted with a lovely tone and freshness of melodic invention; lost to jazz because of a breakdown in the early thirties, after distinguished work with Fletcher Henderson, McKinney, Bessie Smith, and other blues singers.

SMITH, Johnny. GUITAR. B. Birmingham, Ala., 1922. After classical beginnings, Johnny made a kind of languorous ballad line unmistakably his identity in jazz.

SMITH, Paul. PIANO. B. San Diego, Calif., 1922. Fleet, facile modern pianist.

SMITH, Willie. ALTO SAXOPHONE. B. Charleston, S.C., 1908. Lunceford's superb soloist (1930-41), later an ornament of the Harry James and Ellington bands. Also a singer of a simple but distinguished style.

SMITH, Willie "The Lion." PIANO. B. Goshen, N.Y., 1897. A witty speaker, a stride pianist of some skill, and very much a part of New York jazz since the mid-thirties as raconteur and performer.

SOCOLOW, Frankie. TENOR SAXOPHONE. B. Brooklyn, N.Y., 1923. One of the first in the early forties to see the possibilities both of Lester Young and Charlie Parker for big- and small-band jazz.

SOUTH, Eddie. VIOLIN. B. Louisiana, Mo., 1904. Technically expert, possessed of a huge tone and the ability to translate jazz in generous gulps into eloquent fiddle lines.

SPANIER, Francis "Muggsy." CORNET. B. Chicago, Ill., 1906. One of the Chicagoans who has been a durable part of jazz (in spite of a serious illness in New Orleans, 1936-38) right up through the early fifties; a fine plunger performer and always swinging.

SPARGO, Tony. DRUMS. B. New Orleans, La., 1897. An Original Dixieland Jazz Band drummer who lasted up to and including Nicksieland jazz in the fifties.

STACY, Jess. PIANO. B. Cape Girardeau, Mo., 1904. Most famous for his years with Benny Goodman (1935-39), for his effective matching of delicately inflected phrases and a strong beat.

STARK, Bobby. TRUMPET. New York, N.Y., 1906-45. A natural swinging musician, particularly with Fletcher Henderson (1928-29) and Chick Webb (1934-39).

STEWARD, Herbie. TENOR SAXOPHONE. B. Los Angeles, Calif., 1926. One of Woody Herman's "Four Brothers," an early apostle of cool jazz.

STEWART, Rex. CORNET. B. Philadelphia, Pa., 1907. An alternately gutty, "cute," and poignant cornetist whose most effective period (with Duke Ellington, 1934-44) made his half-valve fingerings famous throughout the world.

STEWART, Slam. BASS. B. Englewood, N.J., 1914. One of the wits of jazz in his effective matching of humming and bowing (in octaves).

STITT, Sonny. ALTO SAXOPHONE, TENOR SAXOPHONE. B. Boston, Mass., 1924. One of Charlie Parker's most impressive followers, particularly notable on both instruments for a long, swinging line.

STRAYHORN, Billy. PIANO, ARRANGER. B. Dayton, Ohio, 1915. Since 1939 a most effective composer and arranger for Duke Ellington. Among his swing souvenirs: "Take the 'A' Train" (the Ellington Theme), "Chelsea Bridge," "Johnny Come Lately." As a performer, delicately, lightly Tatumesque.

SULLIVAN, Joe. PIANO. B. Chicago, Ill., 1906. The Chicagoans' keyboard man, much influenced by Hines, very much a part of jazz, chiefly Dixie, right up through the fifties.

TATE, Buddy. TENOR SAXOPHONE. B. Sherman, Texas, 1915. A splendid replacement for Herschel Evans with Count Basie (1939-49), especially in swinging ballads.

TATUM, Art. PIANO. B. Toledo, Ohio, 1910; d. Los Angeles, Calif., 1956. An extraordinary technician who made the most florid phrases fit comfortably into swinging lines, who influenced more jazz musicians than anyone will ever be able to count, and brought to his multiple counter-melodies in performances of pop tunes, salon music, and jazz pieces an abiding elegance never out of place, even with barrelhouse Dixielanders or such straightforwardly groovy musicians as his trio associates in the mid-forties, Tiny Grimes and Slam Stewart.

TAYLOR, Billy, Jr. PIANO. B. Greenville, N.C., 1921. Classically trained keyboard artist who moves from style to style with great ease, but holds his own with such jazz musicians as the boppers, the coolsters, and even more experimental modernists.

TEAGARDEN, Charlie. TRUMPET. B. Vernon, Texas, 1913. An effective performer in the thirties and forties with Ben Pollack, Red Nichols, Paul Whiteman, and brother Jack.

TEAGARDEN, Jack. TROMBONE, SINGER. B. Vernon, Texas, 1905. A thoroughly individual musician with Ben Pollack (1928-33), Paul Whiteman (1934-38), and his own bands, possessor of a natural beat, a lovely mellifluous sound on his horn, and a sense of the jazz phrase which holds one's attention through all kinds of music, even the most meretricious.

TERRY, Clark. TRUMPET. B. St. Louis, Mo., 1920. A fine all-around modernist, a half-valver, one of the best of the Ellington soloists after 1951.

TESCHEMACHER, Frank. CLARINET. B. Kansas City, Mo., 1906; d. Chicago, Ill., 1932. A legendary Chicagoan whose recordings justify the enthusiasm of such contemporaries as Jimmy McPartland for his invention and his beat.

THARPE, Sister Rosetta. SINGER. B. Cotton Plant, Ark., ca. 1905. Of all the folk and folksy singers who have made their way into jazz or any music close to it, this brilliant gospel singer has been consistently the most impressive for her beat, her precise intonation, her natural good taste.

THOMAS, Joseph Lewis. TRUMPET. B. Webster Groves, Mo., 1909. A splendid small-band trumpeter in swing years around New York, particularly effective in middle-register solos.

THOMAS, Joseph Vankert. TENOR SAXOPHONE. B. Uniontown, Pa., 1909. Jimmie Lunceford's booting singer, showman, and tenor star (1932-47).

THOMPSON, Eli "Lucky." TENOR SAXOPHONE. B. Detroit, Mich., 1924. One of the best of those influenced by Hawkins, with a particular ease among boppers, post-boppers, and assorted modernists.

TIZOL, Juan. VALVE TROMBONE, COMPOSER. B. San Juan, Puerto Rico, 1900. Long-time fixture with Ellington (1929-1944, 1951-1953), sometime Harry James musician (1944-1951, 1954-1955), gifted with a fine tone as a soloist and fresh melodic ideas as a composer.

TOUGH, David. DRUMS. B. Oak Park, Ill., 1908; d. Newark, N.J., 1948. The Austin High School gang's intellectual, a brilliantly versatile drummer with Tommy Dorsey, Benny Goodman, and Woody Herman; extraordinarily articulate with sticks or words, remarkably literate, never fazed by any playing problem, and altogether at his ease among Dixielanders, swingsters, boppers, any sort of jazz company.

TRAVIS, Nick. TRUMPET. B. Philadelphia, Pa., 1925. Fine, facile modernist with a number of New York bands, especially Sauter-Finegan in the mid-fifties.

TRISTANO, Lennie. PIANO. B. Chicago, Ill., 1919. Conservatory trained, deeply impressed by Hines and Tatum; after 1946 leader and teacher in New York, experimenting endlessly with combinations of times and tempos, developing musicians like Lee Konitz, Warne Marsh, Arnold Fishkin, and Billy Bauer, not only splendid associates for himself but altogether individual performers for jazz in general. Few have been able to offer such fresh ideas to jazz while preserving the essential free-swinging spirit of the music.

TRUMBAUER, Frank. C MELODY SAXOPHONE. B. Carbondale, Ill., 1900; d. Kansas City, Mo., 1956. An agile performer, indelibly associated with the bands of Jean Goldkette and Paul Whiteman and the records of Bix Beiderbecke, so many of which Trumbauer led from 1927 to 1929.

TURNER, "Big Joe." SINGER. B. Kansas City, Mo., 1911. A superb blues shouter of impeccable intonation and infectious beat, long-lived in jazz.

TWARDZIK, Dick. PIANO. B. Danvers, Mass., 1931; d. Paris, France, 1955. With Charlie Parker, Serge Chaloff, and Chet Baker a modern pianist of considerable freshness and skill.

VAUGHAN, Sarah. SINGER. B. Newark, N.J., 1924. A musicianly singer with Earl Hines (1943-44), Billy Eckstine (1944-45), small groups featuring the boppers, with whom she was closely associated, and all sorts of recording and club outfits. Warmth, precision, and a carefully, consciously developed melodic line characterize her distinguished work, which in the early fifties began to turn farther from jazz, as more and more people came to like what she was doing.

VENTURA, Charlie. TENOR SAXOPHONE, BARITONE SAXOPHONE. B. Philadelphia, Pa., 1916. An effective employer of bop motifs with Gene Krupa (off and on, 1939-46) and his own band (after 1946). Particularly well known for his scoring of unison bop vocals with instruments.

VENUTI, Joe. VIOLIN. B. on ship en route to the United States from Italy, 1904. Perhaps the first jazz fiddler, a fine technician, a witty musician, effective alone, in duets with Eddie Lang, and in various combinations with the musicians of the Goldkette, Whiteman, and Dorsey brothers bands, with whom he recorded.

WALLER, Thomas "Fats." PIANO. B. New York, N.Y., 1904; d. Kansas City, Mo., 1943. A musician of great girth, in every sense of the word, possessed of an overwhelming sense of humor that attacked any unctuous ballad and took audiences by storm or by light wind as Fats' mood demanded. A stride pianist, a delicate balladier when, upon occasion, he took a melody seriously, and a fine leader of sessions, although he rarely recorded or played with musicians of his own high caliber.

WALLINGTON, George. PIANO. B. Palermo, Sicily, 1924. A skillful adapter of bop procedures, a fleet keyboard artist, a thinker at all times, on paper or on his chosen instrument.

WATKINS, Julius. FRENCH HORN. B. Detroit, Mich., 1921. One of the first to turn his instrument loose in jazz, and much in demand on records and for club appearances.

WATSON, Leo. SINGER. B. Kansas City, Mo., 1898; d. Los Angeles, Calif., 1950. Most imaginative of all the scat singers, too little recorded.

WATTERS, Lu. TRUMPET. B. Santa Cruz, Calif., 1911. Leader of a famous New Orleans revival band, the Yerba Buena jazz group, off and on since 1940, chiefly in and around San Francisco.

WAYNE, Chuck. GUITAR. B. New York, N.Y., 1923. A fine post-bopper with a beat, particularly with little bands, many led by him.

WEBB, Chick. DRUMS. Baltimore, Md., 1907-39. A drumming genius who could swing almost any combination of musicians of almost any kind. Leader of a variously distinguished band from 1926 until just before his death. Discoverer of Ella Fitzgerald (1934), a man of remarkable sweetness of disposition and, in spite of a crippling tuberculosis and a deformed figure, absolutely incomparable in his control of all the instruments with which a jazz drummer may surround himself.

WEBSTER, Ben. TENOR SAXOPHONE. B. Kansas City, Mo., 1909. Much experienced, particularly impressive to large numbers of jazz fans with Ellington (1939-43). One of the warmest and most sensitive of performers in the Hawkins tradition and, for all his closeness to Hawk, a distinctly individual tenor man.

WEBSTER, Freddie. TRUMPET. B. Cleveland, Ohio, 1917; d. Chicago, Ill., 1947. A magnificent ballad-playing bopper who gave evidence of becoming one of the great men of modern jazz in the last years of his life in various record dates (especially with Sarah Vaughan) and band engagements (especially with Lucky Millinder and Earl Hines).

WELLS, Dickie. TROMBONE. B. Centerville, Tenn., 1909. A wise and witty musician of the thirties and forties; a man of great verve in the construction of punchy, swinging figures that suggest modern jazz conceptions.

WETTLING, George. DRUMS. B. Topeka, Kan., 1907. A durable Chicagoan, associated with the Nicksieland musicians; also a painter, influenced by Stuart Davis and jazz atmospheres.

WHITEMAN, Paul. LEADER. B. Denver, Colo., 1890. Of particular importance as a sponsor of such jazz musicians as Bix, Venuti and Lang, the Dorseys, Red Norvo and Mildred Bailey, etc.

WILDER, Joe. TRUMPET. B. Colwyn, Pa., 1922. A remarkably adaptable musician who can play almost any kind of music with almost any kind of musician.

WILEY, Lee. SINGER. B. Port Gibson, Okla., 1915. A distinguished singer, closely associated with Dixielanders, but limited to no one school of jazz by her slow, wide vibrato, her keen sense of phrase, her husky warmth.

WILLIAMS, Charles Melvin "Cootie." TRUMPET. B. Mobile, Ala., 1908. Bubber Miley's successor with Duke Ellington (1929-40); his departure from the Duke's ranks to join Benny Goodman was a great loss not only to his former leader but also to himself: thereafter he did not have half as much to say, either as a plunger soloist or as an open trumpeter, as a sideman or as a leader, and in the fifties he had been cut down to the size of a rhythm and blues band leader of little jazz importance.

WILLIAMS, Clarence. PIANO, COMPOSER. B. Plaquemine, La., 1893. Composer of a large number of blues much played in jazz, employer of such musicians as Louis Armstrong and Sidney Bechet, accompanist for such singers as Bessie Smith; generally important for the wealth and breadth of his associations.

WILLIAMS, Joe. SINGER. B. Cordele, Ga., 1918. Basie's booting, round-voiced blues singer of the mid-fifties, capable of endowing almost every sort of vocal line with a contagious lilt.

WILLIAMS, Mary Lou. PIANO, ARRANGER. B. Pittsburgh, Pa., 1910. A brilliantly talented performer and writer of jazz with Andy Kirk (1929-42) and on her own at home and abroad, Mary Lou has progressed along with jazz, sometimes has anticipated some of its most significant developments in her writing or playing or both.

WILLIAMS, Sandy. TROMBONE. B. Somerville, S.C., 1906. Successor to Jimmy Harrison as trombonist's trombonist in the thirties and early forties with Fletcher Henderson and Chick Webb.

WILSON, Dick. TENOR SAXOPHONE. B. Mount Vernon, Ill., 1911; d. New York, N.Y., 1941. Andy Kirk's soft- and sweet-voiced soloist, one of the best balladiers jazz has ever had (1935-41).

WILSON, Gerald. TRUMPET, ARRANGER. B. Shelby, Miss., 1918. A fluent instrumentalist and scripter, one of the first to make good use of modern conceptions in his scores for his own band on the West Coast in the mid-forties and afterward.

WILSON, Teddy. PIANO. B. Austin, Texas, 1912. A great stylist, especially in even-scale, middle-tempo performances, who carried the Earl Hines formulations several steps further, particularly in his left hand chording and the precision of his right-hand melodic lines. Teddy's impressive career has included Chicago bands, among them Erskine Tate, Jimmie Noone, Willie Bryant in New York (1934-35), Benny Goodman (1935-40), and a variety of bands large and small which he himself has led.

WINDING, Kai. TROMBONE. B. Aarhus, Denmark, 1922. One of the best known, most articulate of modernists on his instrument, Kai achieved his reputation with Stan Kenton (1946-47), has been capable of almost every sort of jazz association, but teams up best of all with such bop-inclined performers as J. J. Johnson, with whom he led a band from 1954 to 1956.

WOODS, Phil. ALTO SAXOPHONE. B. Springfield, Mass., 1931. Conservatory-educated, broadly experienced and gifted modernist.

YANCEY, Jimmy. PIANO. Chicago, Ill., 1894-1951. One of the best known of boogie-woogie performers.

YOUNG, James "Trummy." TROMBONE. B. Savannah, Ga., 1912. A witty, swinging showman with Jimmie Lunceford (1937-43) and Louis Armstrong's small band (since 1952).

YOUNG, Lester "Pres." TENOR SAXOPHONE. B. New Orleans, La., 1909. Properly known by everybody with any taste for any sort of modern jazz as "Pres," presiding genius on his instrument, because of the lengthening of lines he achieved, the brilliant use of sustained open notes, the languorous, musically ingenious ballad phrasing, the beat that picked up performance after performance with Count Basie (1936-40) and little bands he has led himself.

ZURKE, Bob. PIANO. B. Detroit, Mich., 1910; d. Los Angeles, Calif., 1944. A fine honky-tonk performer with the Bob Crosby band (1936-39) and as a single.

APPENDIX B

further reading

The literature of jazz has grown in a quarter of a century from a handful of volumes and a small bundle of periodical materials to gigantic proportions. A recent listing of books, magazine references, and magazines wholly or principally devoted to jazz is properly called by its compiler, Robert George Reisner, "a preliminary bibliography." For this publication of the New York Public Library of 1954, although it runs to forty-six double-column pages of titles, does not by any means exhaust the subject. There is some order to be found in this great abundance, however—a natural division according to reader's interest, author's intention, or competence. It is the purpose of these paragraphs to suggest some such division and an orderly way of attacking it.

To begin with, there are the histories and related reference works. My own book, *A History of Jazz in America* (Viking, 1952), is perhaps the most ambitious of those thus far attempted, at least from the point of view of the sheer number of musicians and schools, movements and periods in jazz subjected to examination in a continuous narrative. It can be supplemented today by the present handbook, by Leonard Feather's *Encyclopedia of Jazz* and *Encyclopedia Yearbook of Jazz* (Horizon, 1955, 1956), by the *Metronome Yearbook* (1950 to the present), and the *Down Beat* folio of *Jazz Record Reviews 1956* (first of a series). In all of these can be found special material not always appropriate to a history but essential to the documentation of jazz. Fine texts of the same kind are the Italian *Enciclopedia del Jazz* (Milan: Messiagerie Musicali, 1953) and the Danish *Jazzens Hvem Hvad Hvor* (Copenhagen: Politikens Forlag, 1953).

The testimony of musicians themselves has been gathered by Nat Hentoff and Nat Shapiro into an anthology of absorbing interest, *Hear Me Talkin' to Ya—The Story of Jazz by the Men Who Made It* (Rinehart, 1955). More of the same kind of witness to jazz sounds, sights, and atmospheres can be found in Eddie Condon's entertaining autobiography, *We Called It Music* (Holt, 1947), in W. C. Handy's story of his own life, *Father of the Blues* (Macmillan, 1941), and in Artie Shaw's *The Trouble with Cinderella* (Farrar, Straus and Young, 1952). And in the same category, too, are Louis Armstrong's *Satchmo: My Life in New Orleans* (Prentice-Hall, 1954), Benny Goodman's *The Kingdom of Swing* (Stackpole, 1939), Billie Holiday's *Lady Sings the Blues* (Doubleday, 1956), Milton Mezzrow's *Really the Blues* (Random House, 1946), and Alan Lomax's compilation, *Mister Jelly Roll* (Duell, Sloan and Pearce, 1950). Naturally, these are not disinterested witnesses nor would one want them to be. I must freely confess to my share of special pleading, too, in my biographies, *Duke Ellington* (Creative Age, 1946) and *The Incredible Crosby* (Whittlesey House, 1948).

Another kind of special pleading, more theoretical but not uninfluenced by personalities, is to be found in another set of volumes. The anthropological approach to jazz, emphasizing African origins, is taken by Marshall Stearns in his fluent narrative, *The Story of Jazz* (Oxford University Press, 1956). What has been called the "traditionalist" or "purist" school of jazz history and criticism is represented by a variety of writers in the pioneer work *Jazzmen* (Harcourt, Brace, 1939), by Rudi Blesh in his *Shining Trumpets, a History of Jazz* (Knopf, 1946), and Rex Harris in his historical conspectus *Jazz* (Penguin, 1952). Needless to say, the emphasis in these volumes is heavily upon New Orleans jazz and its practitioners.

There is in these books, as in those of Hugues Panassié, a set of judgments which I find unconvincing, if not arbitrary. If one follows jazz closely, however, or intends to, one should have at least a passing acquaintance with the positions assumed by these critics and historians. As a balance, corrective or not, I should recommend the analytical essays in André Hodeir's *Jazz: Its Evolution and Essence* (Grove, 1956), the provocative distinctions made between "the Christian element" and "secular elements" in New Orleans jazz in the opening chapters of *The Heart of Jazz* by William L. Grossman (New York University, 1956), and the various discussions, controversies, and critical pieces that enliven the pages of jazz periodicals.

In this country today the chronicle of jazz is kept up to

date on a bi-weekly basis by *Down Beat,* monthly by *Metro-nome, Jazz Today,* and *The Record Changer.* The first mixes news and opinion about equally. The others, because of deadline requirements, lean more to opinion. There are other magazines at least worth glancing at, English (*Melody Maker, New Musical Express,* and *Jazz Journal*), French (*Jazz Hot* and *Jazz Magazine*), Italian (*Musica Jazz*), and Swedish (*Estrad* and *Orkester Journalen*).

One would like to be able to finish up this discussion with a warm recommendation of at least two or three jazz novels or related works of the imagination. Unfortunately, although there have been many attempts to translate the spirit, the environment, and the personalities of jazz into novel and film, one can point only to a short story by Elliott Grennard, "Sparrow's Last Jump," a thinly disguised portrait of the late Charlie Parker in one of his more anguished moments; some of the descriptive writing in *Young Man with a Horn,* Doro-thy Baker's portrait of Bix Beiderbecke—long but not full-length; a short film, *Jammin' the Blues;* and the backgrounds supplied to some motion pictures, whether about jazz or not, by the West Coast school and a few specially hired national names. For the present, the only altogether successful rela-tionship between jazz and the faculties of the creative imagi-nation is the direct one. Perhaps that is as it should be.

a comparative chronology of jazz and other arts in the twentieth century

YEAR	JAZZ	OTHER MUSIC	THEATER AND FILM	LITERATURE	PAINTING
1900	Jack Laine's Ragtime Band	Rachmaninoff: C minor Piano Concerto		D'Annunzio: *The Flame of Life*	
1901				Kipling: *Kim*	
1902	Jelly Roll Morton plays in Storyville	Sibelius: *Second Symphony*; Debussy: *Pelléas and Mélisande*	Strindberg: *A Dream Play*; *A Trip to the Moon* (dir. Méliès)	Conrad: *Heart of Darkness*	
1903			*The Great Train Robbery* (dir. Porter)	Butler: *The Way of All Flesh*; James: *The Ambassadors*	
1904		Puccini: *Madame Butterfly*	Chekhov: *The Cherry Orchard*	Hudson: *Green Mansions*	
1905		Strauss: *Salome*			"Les Fauves"—Vlaminck, Derain, Matisse, etc.
1906			Kinemacolor (first color films)		Cézanne dies; homage and imitation ensue
1907		Delius: *Brigg Fair*	Synge: *The Playboy of the Western World*		Picasso: *The Ladies of Avignon*
1908	Olympia Band (with Keppard and Picou)	Mahler: *The Song of the Earth*		Stein: *Three Lives*	Picasso and Braque launch Cubism
1909				Wells: *Tono-Bungay*	Marinetti's Manifesto of Futurism
1910	Papa Celestin at the Tuxedo Hall; Kid Ory's Brownskin Babies	Rimsky-Korsakov: *The Golden Cockerel*			Rousseau: *The Dream*

YEAR	JAZZ	OTHER MUSIC	THEATER AND FILM	LITERATURE	PAINTING
1911	Original Creole Band (with Keppard) tours; Eagle Band (with Bunk Johnson)	Berlin: "Alexander's Ragtime Band"		Wharton: *Ethan Frome*	Braque: *Man with a Guitar*
1912		Schönberg: *Pierrot Lunaire*; Ravel: *Daphnis and Chloé*	*The New York Hat* (Mary Pickford, Lionel Barrymore)		Duchamp: *Nude Descending a Staircase*; "The Blue Riders"— Klee, Kandinsky, etc.
1913	Louis Armstrong sent to Waifs' Home	Stravinsky: *The Rite of Spring*		First volumes of Proust's *Remembrance of Things Past*; Lawrence: *Sons and Lovers*	New York Armory Show introduces new movements to U.S.
1914				Frost: *North of Boston*	De Chirico: *Nostalgia of the Infinite*
1915	Tom Brown's Dixieland Jass Band in Chicago	Falla: *El Amor Brujo*	*The Birth of a Nation* (dir. Griffith)	Maugham: *Of Human Bondage*	
1916		Bloch: *Schelomo*	*Intolerance* (dir. Griffith)		Dadaism makes its bow
1917	First records of Original Dixieland Jazz Band; Storyville closed				
1918	Louis Armstrong with Fate Marable's riverboat band; King Oliver in Chicago	Prokofiev: "Classical" Symphony	Kaiser: *Gas*	Hopkins' *Poems* (posthumous); Blok: *The Twelve*	Malevich: *White on White*

YEAR	JAZZ	OTHER MUSIC	THEATER AND FILM	LITERATURE	PAINTING
1919			The Cabinet of Dr. Caligari (Werner Krauss)	Anderson: Winesburg, Ohio	Bauhaus established; Léger: The City
1920	New Orleans Rhythm Kings in Chicago	Berg: Wozzeck		Lewis: Main Street; Pound: Hugh Selwyn Mauberley; Hamsun: Growth of the Soil	
1921			Capek: R.U.R.; The Sheik (Rudolph Valentino)		Picasso: Three Musicians
1922	Louis Armstrong joins King Oliver at the Lincoln Gardens; Austin High School Gang forms; Fletcher Henderson in New York	Carpenter: Krazy Kat		Eliot: The Wasteland; Joyce: Ulysses; Rilke: Duino Elegies	Marin: Lower Manhattan; Klee: Twittering Machine
1923	Bennie Moten leads Kansas City band on records; Bessie Smith makes first records	Walton: Façade; Milhaud: The Creation of the World	Shaw: Saint Joan; The Covered Wagon (dir. Cruze)		
1924	Louis Armstrong with Henderson; Bix Beiderbecke joins the Wolverines	Gershwin: Rhapsody in Blue; Honegger: Pacific 231	O'Casey: Juno and the Paycock; The Navigator (Buster Keaton)	Forster: A Passage to India; Mann: The Magic Mountain	André Breton's Manifesto of Surrealism
1925	Louis Armstrong's Hot Five; Bix and Trumbauer together	Bartok: Fourth Quartet; Gruenberg: Daniel Jazz	Potemkin (dir. Eisenstein); The Gold Rush (Charles Chaplin)	Fitzgerald: The Great Gatsby; Kafka's The Trial; Gide: The Counterfeiters	Hopper: House by the Railroad

YEAR	JAZZ	OTHER MUSIC	THEATER AND FILM	LITERATURE	PAINTING
1926	Bix with Jean Goldkette; Red Nichols' Five Pennies record		*What Price Glory?* (Edmund Lowe, Victor McLaglen)	Hemingway: *The Sun Also Rises*	Miró: *Person Throwing a Stone at a Bird*
1927	Jimmie Noone, Earl Hines at the Apex Club, Chicago; Duke Ellington at the Cotton Club, New York	Krenek: *Jonny spielt auf* ("a jazz opera")	*The Jazz Singer* (Al Jolson)	Woolf: *To the Lighthouse*; Yeats: *The Tower*	
1928	Don Redman joins McKinney's Cotton Pickers; first boogie-woogie era	Weill: *Threepenny Opera*	*The Way of All Flesh* (Emil Jannings)	Huxley: *Point Counter Point*	
1929	So-called "Harlem Jazz" takes shape; jazz of quality under Benny Carter, Luis Russell, etc.	Kern and Hammerstein: *Show Boat*	Claudel: *The Satin Slipper*; *Hallelujah* (dir. Vidor)	Faulkner: *The Sound and the Fury*; Wolfe: *Look Homeward, Angel*	
1930	Jazz a back-room music as result of depression		*All Quiet on the Western Front* (dir. Milestone)	Waugh: *Vile Bodies*	Wood: *American Gothic*
1931	Don Redman leads own band	Varèse: *Ionisation*	O'Neill: *Mourning Becomes Electra*		Dali: *The Persistence of Memory*
1932	Louis Armstrong's first European tour	Porter: *The Gay Divorce*		Mauriac: *Vipers' Tangle*	
1933	Duke Ellington band to Europe		Garcia Lorca: *Blood Wedding*	Malraux: *Man's Fate*	Matisse: *Dance* mural for Barnes Foundation, Merion, Pa.

YEAR	JAZZ	OTHER MUSIC	THEATER AND FILM	LITERATURE	PAINTING
1934	Dorsey Brothers Band forms; Panassié's book *Le Jazz Hot*; Jimmie Lunceford band develops style and influence	Hindemith: *Mathias the Painter*; Thomson and Stein: *Four Saints in Three Acts*	Cocteau: *The Infernal Machine*; *Chapayev* (dir. Vasilyev)	O'Hara: *Appointment in Samarra*	
1935	Benny Goodman band organized; the Dorseys split, form two bands; Ella Fitzgerald joins Chick Webb; Teddy Wilson record dates with Billie Holiday	Gershwin: *Porgy and Bess*	Eliot: *Murder in the Cathedral*; *The Informer* (Victor McLaglen)		
1936	Kansas City jazz flourishes: Basie and Kirk (with Mary Lou Williams); Woody Herman, Artie Shaw organize	Prokofiev: *Peter and the Wolf*	*Modern Times* (Charlie Chaplin); *Camille* (Greta Garbo)	Silone: *Bread and Wine*	Rouault: *The Old King*
1937	Small bands great success, on and off records: Bob Crosby's Bob Cats, Lionel Hampton, etc.	Copland: *El Salon Mexico*	Giraudoux: *Electra*; *Grand Illusion* (Pierre Fresnay, Erich von Stroheim)		Picasso: *Guernica*; Braque: *Woman with a Mandolin*
1938	Benny Goodman at Carnegie Hall; boogie woogie revived (Carnegie); John Kirby, Gene Krupa bands	Rodgers and Hart: *The Boys from Syracuse*	*Snow White and the Seven Dwarfs* (prod. Disney)	Baker: *Young Man with a Horn*; Dos Passos: *U. S. A.*	

YEAR	JAZZ	OTHER MUSIC	THEATER AND FILM	LITERATURE	PAINTING
1939	Goodman Sextet features Charlie Christian; Harry James, Jack Teagarden, Teddy Wilson bands		Barry: The Philadelphia Story	Joyce: Finnegans Wake	
1940	Duke Ellington features Blanton and Webster; Calloway features Chu Berry; Charlie Parker with Jay McShann		The Baker's Wife (Raimu)	Greene: The Power and the Glory	
1941	Bebop takes shape at Minton's sessions; Stan Kenton organizes			Koestler: Darkness at Noon	Tamayo: Animals
1942	Jazz at the Philharmonic tours begin	Shostakovitch: "Leningrad" Symphony	Anouilh: Antigone		
1943	Boppers with Earl Hines (Bird, Dizzy, Sarah Vaughan) and Andy Kirk (Howard McGhee, Fats Navarro); Ellington's Black, Brown and Beige (at Carnegie Hall)	Messaien: Visions de l'Amen		Eliot: Four Quartets	Mondrian: Broadway Boogie Woogie
1944	Bop sessions and bop bands on 52nd Street; Art Tatum Trio; New Orleans revival		Sartre: No Exit		

YEAR	JAZZ	OTHER MUSIC	THEATER AND FILM	LITERATURE	PAINTING
1945	Dizzy and Bird together; Woody Herman arrives (with Flip Phillips, Bill Harris, Chubby Jackson, etc.)	Britten: *Peter Grimes*			
1946	Lennie Tristano Trio; Woody Herman at Carnegie (Stravinsky's *Ebony Concerto*)	Menotti: *The Medium*	*Open City* (dir. Rossellini)	Thomas: *Deaths and Entrances*	
1947	Parker Quintet with Miles Davis, Max Roach; Woody's "Four Brothers" band		Williams: *A Streetcar Named Desire*	Camus: *The Plague*	
1948	Jazz Festival at Nice, France	Vaughan Williams: Sixth Symphony; Schönberg: *A Survivor of Warsaw*			Pollock: *Number 1*
1949	Cool jazz flourishes; Miles Davis's Capitol sides; Afro-Cuban fashion; Jazz Festival at Paris	Rodgers and Hammerstein: *South Pacific*	Miller: *Death of a Salesman*; Fry: *The Lady's Not for Burning*	Orwell: *1984*	Picasso's dove for Congress of Partisans of Peace
1950	Brubeck Octet and Trio and Quartet; Red Norvo Trio; Kenton "Innovations" tour				
1951	Swedish jazz captures interest of Americans	Stravinsky: *The Rake's Progress*			Matisse: Chapel at Vence, France

238

YEAR	JAZZ	OTHER MUSIC	THEATER AND FILM	LITERATURE	PAINTING
1952	Gerry Mulligan Quartet		Cinerama (and other three-dimensional film processes)		De Kooning: *Woman, I*
1953	Benny Goodman revives 1936 band			Gironella: *The Cypresses Believe in God*	
1954	First Newport Jazz Festival		*On the Waterfront* (dir. Kazan)		Dubuffet: *Eyes Closed*
1955	Modern Jazz Quartet, Charlie Mingus groups typical of new jazz era	Rock 'n' Roll hysteria	Posthumous production of O'Neill's *Long Day's Journey into Night*; Beckett: *Waiting for Godot*		
1956	Neo-Classical movement; experimental jazz flourishes; Dizzy Gillespie, Benny Goodman bands tour East; Stratford (Ontario) Festival features jazz	Lerner and Loewe: *My Fair Lady*	*Around the World in Eighty Days* (dir. Anderson)		
1957	Ellington's *A Drum Is a Woman*				

index